POCKET REFERENCE

*GMAT is a registered trademark of the Graduate Management Admission Council. Kaplan materials do not contain actual GMAT items and are neither endorsed by nor affiliated in any way with GMAC.

TEST PREP

Special thanks to the team that worked on the 2010 revision of this book:

Tajinder Ahluwalia, Arthur Ahn, Rashid Akhter, Joshua Allen, Paul Allen, Gina Allison, Sanmati Ananthamurthy, Alisun Armstrong, Daniel Bachmann, Doug Barg, Kevin Bedeau, Greg Bollinger, Alix Bowman, Bevin Bullock, Jennifer Burbage, Keron Chang, Robert Colpitts, Chris Combs, Junel S. Corales, Charlie Corona, Priya Dasgupta-Yeung, Elisa Davis, Erin Decker, Okan Demirmen, Neelam Desai, Kevin Doherty, Peter Drew, Chris Dye, Alyson Fitch, Paula Fleming, Brian Fruchey, Darcy Galane, Devu Gandhi, Karuppiah Ganesan, Robert Garrelick, Susan Gaunt, Phil Glick, Ronny Gonzalez, Joanna Graham, Adam Grey, Zoya Grigoryan, Candi Halbert, Adel Hanash, Moinul Haque, Kristin Henke, Kashif Heyat, John Hightower, Jeannie Ho, Chip Hurlburt, Cinzia Iacono, Dzmitry Ivanou, Jyoti Jeerage, Ben John, Clint Jusino, Burton Kagen, Jennifer Kedrowski, Michael Kellman, Chris Koeberle, Joanne L'Abbate, Devin Landin, Matthew Landin, Carolyn Landis, Ben Leff, Aaron Lemon-Strauss, David Lorenc, Richard Lorenzo, Keith Lubeley, Jennifer Lynch, Glenn Maciag, Sameer Mandavia, Ania Maniara, Adam Maze, Danielle Mazza, Asim McArthur, Antoineta McCrea, Shana McCullough, Paul McNair, Loren Mendelsohn, Matthew Merson, Eli Meyer, Andrew Mitchell, Claire Molloy, Jennifer Moore, Todd Morgan, Jason Moss, Swapna Muppidi, Naveen Myangar, Rajesh Natarajan, Maria Nicholas, Walt Niedner, Deborah Osborn, Krunal Patel, Kojo Pilgrim, Shoshana Pfeiffer, Lisa Plante, Loretta Pontillo, Carl Pyrdum, Prasanna Rajagopalan, Robert Reiss, Damali Rhett, Ariane Root, Bret Ruber, Brigid Ryan, Marc SanLuis, Dustin Semo, Maulik Shah, Sahithi Sharma, Lori Shriner, Lauren Siliati, Alexander Smith, Murl Smith, Stephen Snyder, Toni Spinozzi, Oliver Stewart, Glen Stohr, Lisa Stringer, Edwin Suarez, Joe Suchta, Gene Suhir, Matthew Sullivan, Matthew Thomas, Stephanie Thompson, Anthony Todd, Barry Tonoff, Martha Torres, Eric Turner, Michael Valaire, Alan Varghese, Bob Verini, Charles Vu, Liza Weale, Stephen Weichsel, Philip Wells, Omar Williams, Dennis Yim, Nina Yoh, Todd York, Matt Zaller, Mike Zandlo, Max Zener

© 2012 Kaplan, Inc.

All rights reserved. No part of this book may be reproduced or transmitted in any form or by any means, electronic, or mechanical, including photocopying, recording, or by any information storage and retrieval system, without the express written consent of Kaplan, Inc., except where permitted by law.

TABLE OF CONTENTS

Part One: Math Reference

Chapter 1: Arithmetic 1

Chapter 2: Number Properties 9

Chapter 3: Proportions and Math Formulas 29

Chapter 4: Algebra 71

Chapter 5: Statistics 95

Chapter 6: Geometry 107

Chapter 7: Other Topics 157

Part Two: Grammar Reference

Chapter 8: Sentence Structure 169

Chapter 9: Subject-Verb Agreement 175

Chapter 10: Modification 183

Chapter 11: Pronouns 189

Chapter 12: Verbs 201

Chapter 13: Parallelism 213

Chapter 14: Comparisons 219

Chapter 15: Ellipsis 223

Chapter 16: Style 227

Chapter 17: Commonly Misused Words 231

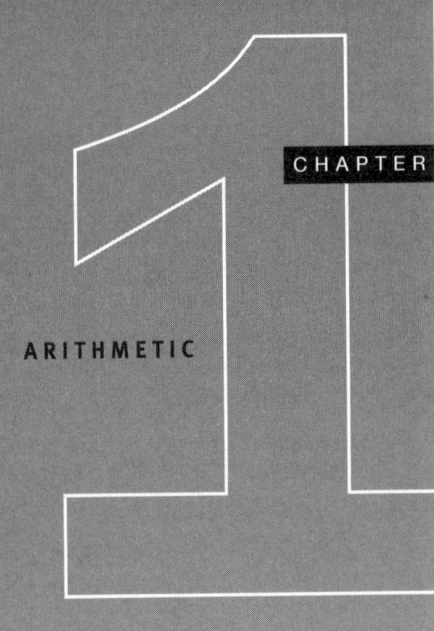

CHAPTER 1

ARITHMETIC

CHAPTER 1

Terms

Consecutive numbers: Numbers of a certain type, following one another without interruption. Numbers may be consecutive in ascending or descending direction. The GMAT prefers to test consecutive integers (e.g., $-2, -1, 0, 1, 2, 3 \ldots$), but you may encounter other types of consecutive numbers. For example:

$-4, -2, 0, 2, 4, 6, \ldots$ is a series of consecutive even numbers.

$-3, 0, 3, 6, 9, \ldots$ is a series of consecutive multiples of 3.

$2, 3, 5, 7, 11, \ldots$ is a series of consecutive prime numbers.

Cube: A number raised to the 3rd power. For example $4^3 = (4)(4)(4) = 64$, and 64 is the cube of 4.

Decimal: A fraction written in decimal system format. For example, 0.6 is a decimal. To convert a fraction to a decimal, divide the numerator by the denominator.

Decimal system: A numbering system based on the powers of 10. The decimal system is the only numbering system used on the GMAT. Each figure, or digit, in a decimal number occupies a particular position, from which it derives its place value.

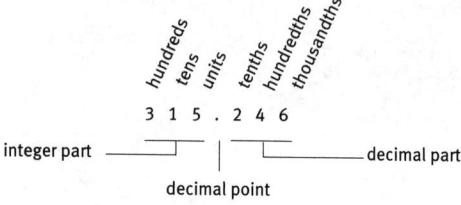

CHAPTER 1

Denominator: The quantity in the bottom of a fraction, representing the whole.

Difference: The result of subtraction.

Digit: One of the numerals 0, 1, 2, 3, 4, 5, 6, 7, 8, or 9. A number can have several digits. For example, the number 542 has three digits: a 5, a 4, and a 2. The number 321,321,000 has nine digits, but only four distinct (different) digits: 3, 2, 1, and 0.

Element: One of the members of a set.

Exponent: The number that denotes the power to which another number or variable is raised. The exponent is typically written as a superscript to a number. For example, 5^3 equals $(5)(5)(5)$. The exponent is also occasionally referred to as a "power." For example, 5^3 can be described as "5 to the 3rd power." The product, 125, is "the 3rd power of 5."

Fraction: The division of a part by a whole. $\frac{\text{Part}}{\text{Whole}} = \text{Fraction}$. For example, $\frac{3}{5}$ is a fraction.

Integer: A number without fractional or decimal parts, including negative whole numbers and zero. All integers are multiples of 1. The following are examples of integers: $-5, -4, -3, -2, -1, 0, 1, 2, 3, 4, 5$.

Number line: A straight line, extending infinitely in either direction, on which numbers are represented as points. The number line below shows the integers from -3 to 4. Decimals and fractions can also be depicted on a number line, as can irrational numbers, such as $\sqrt{2}$.

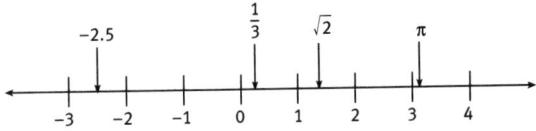

ARITHMETIC

CHAPTER 1

The values of numbers get larger as you move to the right along the number line. Numbers to the right of zero are *positive*; numbers to the left of zero are *negative*. **Zero is neither positive nor negative.** Any positive number is larger than any negative number. For example, $-300 < 4$.

Numerator: The quantity in the top of the fraction, representing the part.

Operation: A function or process performed on one or more numbers. The four basic arithmetic operations are addition, subtraction, multiplication, and division.

Part: A specified number of the equal sections that comprise a whole.

Product: The result of multiplication.

Set: A well-defined collection of items, typically numbers, objects, or events. The bracket symbols { } are normally used to define sets of numbers. For example, {2, 4, 6, 8} is a set of numbers.

Square: The product of a number multiplied by itself. A squared number has been raised to the 2nd power. For example, $4^2 = (4)(4) = 16$, and 16 is the square of 4.

Sum: The result of addition.

Whole: A quantity that is regarded as a complete unit.

CHAPTER 1

Symbols

- $=$ is equal to
- $\neq$ is not equal to
- $<$ is less than
- $>$ is greater than
- $\leq$ is less than or equal to
- $\geq$ is greater than or equal to
- $\div$ divided by
- π pi (the ratio of the circumference of a circle to the diameter)
- $\pm$ plus or minus
- $\sqrt{}$ square root
- $\angle$ angle

CHAPTER

1

Rules of Operation

There are certain mathematical laws governing the results of the four basic operations: addition, subtraction, multiplication, and division. Although you won't need to know the names of these laws for the GMAT, you'll benefit from understanding them.

PEMDAS

A string of operations must be performed in proper order. The acronym PEMDAS stands for the correct order of operations:

Parentheses

Exponents

Multiplication
Division } simultaneously from left to right

Addition
Subtraction } simultaneously from left to right

If you have trouble remembering PEMDAS, you can think of the mnemonic "Please Excuse My Dear Aunt Sally."

Example:

$66 (3 - 2) \div 11$

If you were to perform all the operations sequentially from left to right, without using PEMDAS, you would arrive at an answer of $\frac{196}{11}$. But if you perform the operation within the parentheses first, you get $66(1) \div 11 = 66 \div 11 = 6$, which is the correct answer.

CHAPTER 1

Example:

$$30 - 5(4) + \frac{(7-3)^2}{8}$$
$$= 30 - 5(4) + \frac{4^2}{8}$$
$$= 30 - 5(4) + \frac{16}{8}$$
$$= 30 - 20 + 2$$
$$= 10 + 2$$
$$= 12$$

Commutative Laws of Addition and Multiplication

Addition and multiplication are both commutative; switching the order of any two numbers being added or multiplied together does not affect the result.

Example:

$5 + 8 = 8 + 5$

$(2)(3)(6) = (6)(3)(2)$

$a + b = b + a$

$ab = ba$

Division and subtraction are not commutative; switching the order of the numbers changes the result. For instance, $3 - 2 \neq 2 - 3$; the left side yields a difference of 1, while the right side yields a difference of -1. Similarly, $\frac{6}{2} \neq \frac{2}{6}$; the left side equals 3, while the right side equals $\frac{1}{3}$.

ARITHMETIC

CHAPTER 1

Associative Laws of Addition and Multiplication

Addition and multiplication are also associative; regrouping the numbers does not affect the result.

Example:

$$(3 + 5) + 8 = 3 + (5 + 8) \qquad (a + b) + c = a + (b + c)$$
$$8 + 8 = 3 + 13 \qquad\qquad\qquad (ab)c = a(bc)$$
$$16 = 16$$

The Distributive Law

In multiplication, the distributive law of multiplication allows you to "distribute" a factor over numbers that are added or subtracted. You do this by multiplying that factor by each number in the group.

Example:

$$4(3 + 7) = (4)(3) + (4)(7) \qquad a(b + c) = ab + ac$$
$$4(10) = 12 + 28$$
$$40 = 40$$

The law works for the numerator in division as well.

$$\frac{a + b}{c} = \frac{a}{c} + \frac{b}{c}$$

However, when the sum or difference is in the denominator—that is, when you're dividing by a sum or difference—no distribution is possible.

$\frac{9}{4 + 5}$ is *not* equal to $\frac{9}{4} + \frac{9}{5}$.

ARITHMETIC

NUMBER PROPERTIES

CHAPTER 2

CHAPTER

2

Adding and Subtracting

Numbers can be treated as though they have two parts: a positive or negative sign and a number. Numbers without any sign are understood to be positive.

To add two numbers that have the same sign, add the number parts and keep the sign. Example: To add $(-6) + (-3)$, add 6 and 3 and then attach the negative sign from the original numbers to the sum: $(-6) + (-3) = -9$.

To add two numbers that have different signs, find the difference between the number parts and keep the sign of the number whose number part is larger. Example: To add $(-7) + (+4)$, subtract 4 from 7 to get 3. Because $7 > 4$ (the number part of -7 is greater than the number part of 4), the final sum will be negative: $(-7) + (+4) = -3$.

Subtraction is the opposite of addition. You can rephrase any subtraction problem as an addition problem by changing the operation sign from a minus to a plus and switching the sign on the second number. Example: $8 - 5 = 8 + (-5)$. There's no real advantage to rephrasing if you are subtracting a smaller positive number from a larger positive number. But the concept comes in very handy when you are subtracting a negative number from any other number, a positive number from a negative number, or a larger positive number from a smaller positive number.

To subtract a negative number, rephrase as an addition problem and follow the rules for addition of signed numbers. For instance, $9 - (-10) = 9 + 10 = 19$.

To subtract a positive number from a negative number, or from a smaller positive number, change the sign of the number that you are subtracting from positive to negative and follow the rules for addition of signed numbers. For example, $(-4) - 1 = (-4) + (-1) = -5$.

CHAPTER 2

Multiplication and Division of Signed Numbers

Multiplying or dividing two numbers with the same sign gives a positive result.

Examples:

$(-4)(-7) = +28$

$(-50) \div (-5) = +10$

Multiplying or dividing two numbers with different signs gives a negative result.

Examples:

$(-2)(+3) = -6$

$8 \div (-4) = -2$

CHAPTER 2

Absolute Value

The absolute value of a number is the value of a number without its sign. It is written as two vertical lines, one on either side of the number and its sign.

Example:

$|-3| = |+3| = 3$

The absolute value of a number can be thought of as the number's distance from zero on the number line. Since both 3 and -3 are 3 units from 0, each has an absolute value of 3. If you are told that $|x| = 5$, x could equal 5 or -5.

CHAPTER 2

Properties of Zero

Adding zero to or subtracting zero from a number does not change the number.

$$x + 0 = x$$
$$0 + x = x$$
$$x - 0 = x$$

Examples:

$5 + 0 = 5$

$0 + (-3) = -3$

$4 - 0 = 4$

Notice, however, that subtracting a number from zero changes the number's sign. It's easy to see why if you rephrase the problem as an addition problem.

Example:

Subtract 5 from 0.

$0 - 5 = -5$. That's because $0 - 5 = 0 + (-5)$, and according to the rules for addition with signed numbers, $0 + (-5) = -5$.

CHAPTER 2

The product of zero and any number is zero.

Examples:

$(0)(z) = 0$

$(z)(0) = 0$

$(0)(12) = 0$

Division by zero is undefined. For GMAT purposes, that translates as "it can't be done." Since fractions are essentially division (that is, $\frac{1}{4}$ means $1 \div 4$), any fraction with zero in the denominator is also undefined. So when you are given a fraction that has an algebraic expression in the denominator, be sure that the expression cannot equal zero.

Properties of 1 and −1

Multiplying or dividing a number by 1 does not change the number.

$$(a)(1) = a$$
$$(1)(a) = a$$
$$a \div 1 = a$$

Examples:

$(4)(1) = 4$

$(1)(-5) = -5$

$(-7) \div 1 = -7$

Multiplying or dividing a nonzero number by −1 changes the sign of the number.

$$(a)(-1) = -a$$
$$(-1)(a) = -a$$
$$a \div (-1) = -a$$

Examples:

$(6)(-1) = -6$

$(-3)(-1) = 3$

$(-8) \div (-1) = 8$

CHAPTER

2

Factors, Multiples, and Remainders

Multiples and Divisibility

A multiple is the product of a specified number and an integer. For example, 3, 12, and 90 are all multiples of 3: 3 = (3)(1); 12 = (3)(4); and 90 = (3)(30). The number 4 is not a multiple of 3, because there is no integer that can be multiplied by 3 and yield 4.

The concepts of multiples and factors are tied together by the idea of divisibility. A number is said to be evenly divisible by another number if the result of the division is an integer with no remainder. A number that is evenly divisible by a second number is also a multiple of the second number.

For example, 52 ÷ 4 = 13, which is an integer. So 52 is evenly divisible by 4, and it's also a multiple of 4.

On some GMAT math problems, you will find yourself trying to assess whether one number is evenly divisible by another. You can use several simple rules to save time.

- An integer is divisible by 2 if its last digit is divisible by 2.
- An integer is divisible by 3 if its digits add up to a multiple of 3.
- An integer is divisible by 4 if its last two digits are a multiple of 4.
- An integer is divisible by 5 if its last digit is 0 or 5.
- An integer is divisible by 6 if it is divisible by 2 and 3.
- An integer is divisible by 9 if its digits add up to a multiple of 9.

CHAPTER 2

Example:

6,930 is a multiple of 2, since 0 is even.

... a multiple of 3, since 6 + 9 + 3 + 0 = 18, which is a multiple of 3.

... not a multiple of 4, since 30 is not a multiple of 4.

... a multiple of 5, since it ends in zero.

... a multiple of 6, since it is a multiple of 2 and 3.

... a multiple of 9, since 6 + 9 + 3 + 0 = 18, a multiple of 9.

Properties of Odd/Even Numbers

Even numbers are integers that are evenly divisible by 2; *odd* numbers are integers that are not evenly divisible by 2. Integers whose last digit is 0, 2, 4, 6, or 8 are even; integers whose last digit is 1, 3, 5, 7, or 9 are odd. The terms *odd* and *even* apply only to integers, but they may be used for either positive or negative integers. 0 is considered even.

Rules for Odds and Evens

Odd + Odd = Even

Even + Even = Even

Odd + Even = Odd

Odd × Odd = Odd

Even × Even = Even

Odd × Even = Even

Note that multiplying any even number by *any* integer always produces another even number.

CHAPTER

2

It may be easier to pick numbers in problems that ask you to decide whether some unknown will be odd or even.

Example:

Is the sum of two odd numbers odd or even?

Pick any two odd numbers, for example, 3 and 5. $3 + 5 = 8$. Since the sum of the two odd numbers that you picked is an even number, 8, it's safe to say that the sum of any two odd numbers is even.

Picking Numbers will work in any odds/evens problem, no matter how complicated. The only time you have to be careful is when division is involved, especially if the problem is in Data Sufficiency format; different numbers may yield different results.

Example:

Integer x is evenly divisible by 2. Is $\frac{x}{2}$ even?

By definition, any multiple of 2 is even, so integer x is even. And $\frac{x}{2}$ must be an integer. But is $\frac{x}{2}$ even or odd? In this case, picking two different even numbers for x can yield two different results. If you let $x = 4$, then $\frac{x}{2} = \frac{4}{2} = 2$ which is even. But if you let $x = 6$, then $\frac{x}{2} = \frac{6}{2} = 3$, which is odd. So $\frac{x}{2}$ could be even or odd—and you wouldn't know that if you picked only one number.

CHAPTER 2

Factors and Primes

The *factors*, or *divisors*, of an integer are the positive integers by which it is evenly divisible (leaving no remainder).

Example:

What are the factors of 36?

36 has nine factors: 1, 2, 3, 4, 6, 9, 12, 18, and 36. We can group these factors in pairs: (1)(36) = (2)(18) = (3)(12) = (4)(9) = (6)(6).

The *greatest common factor*, or greatest common divisor, of a pair of integers is the largest factor that they share.

To find the greatest common factor, break down both integers into their prime factorizations and multiply all the prime factors they have in common: 36 = (2)(2)(3)(3), and 48 = (2)(2)(2)(2)(3). What they have in common is two 2s and one 3, so the GCF is (2)(2)(3) = 12.

A prime number is an integer greater than 1 that has only two factors: itself and 1. The number 1 is not considered a prime, because it is divisible only by itself. The number 2 is the smallest prime number and the only even prime. (Any other even number must have 2 as a factor and therefore cannot be prime.)

Prime Factors

The prime factorization of a number is the expression of the number as the product of its prime factors (the factors that are prime numbers).

CHAPTER 2

There are two common ways to determine a number's prime factorization. The rules given above for determining divisibility by certain numbers come in handy in both methods.

Method #1: Work your way up through the prime numbers, starting with 2. (You'll save time in this process, especially when you're starting with a large number, by knowing the first ten prime numbers by heart: 2, 3, 5, 7, 11, 13, 17, 19, 23, and 29.)

Example:

What is the prime factorization of 210?

$$210 = (2)(105)$$

Since 105 is odd, it can't contain another factor of 2. The next smallest prime number is 3. The digits of 105 add up to 6, which is a multiple of 3, so 3 is a factor of 105.

$$210 = (2)(3)(35)$$

The digits of 35 add up to 8, which is not a multiple of 3. But 35 ends in 5, so it is a multiple of the next largest prime number, 5.

$$210 = (2)(3)(5)(7)$$

Since 7 is a prime number, this equation expresses the complete prime factorization of 210.

Method #2: Figure out one pair of factors, and then determine their factors, continuing the process until you're left with only prime numbers. Those primes will be the prime factorization.

CHAPTER 2

Example:

What is the prime factorization of 1,050?

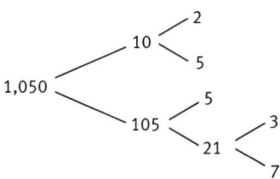

The discrete prime factors of 1,050 are therefore 2, 5, 3, and 7, with the prime number 5 occurring twice in the prime factorization. We usually write out the prime factorization by putting the prime numbers in increasing order. Here, that would be (2)(3)(5)(5)(7). The prime factorization can also be expressed in exponential form: $(2)(3)(5^2)(7)$.

The Least Common Multiple

The *least common multiple* of two or more integers is the smallest number that is a multiple of each of the integers. Here's one quick way to find it:

(1) Determine the prime factorization of each integer.
(2) Write out each prime number the maximum number of times that it appears in any one of the prime factorizations.
(3) Multiply those prime numbers together to get the least common multiple of the original integers.

CHAPTER 2

Example:

What is the least common multiple of 6 and 8?

Start by finding the prime factors of 6 and 8.

$$6 = (2)(3)$$
$$8 = (2)(2)(2)$$

The factor 2 appears three times in the prime factorization of 8, while 3 appears as only a single factor of 6. So the least common multiple of 6 and 8 will be (2)(2)(2)(3), or 24.

Note that the least common multiple of two integers is smaller than their product if they have any factors in common. For instance, the product of 6 and 8 is 48, but their least common multiple is only 24.

Although you won't see the term *least common multiple* very often on the GMAT, you'll find the concept useful whenever you're adding or subtracting fractions with different denominators.

Remainders

The remainder is what is "left over" in a division problem. A remainder is always smaller than the number you are dividing by. For instance, 17 divided by 3 is 5, with a remainder of 2. Likewise, 12 divided by 6 is 2, with a remainder of 0 (since 12 is evenly divisible by 6).

GMAT writers often disguise remainder problems. For instance, a problem might state that the slats of a fence are painted in three colors, which appear in a fixed order, such as red, yellow, blue, red, yellow, blue. You would then be asked something like, "If the first slat is red, what color is the 301st slat?" Since 3 goes into 300 evenly, the whole pattern must finish on the 300th slat and start all over again on the 301st. Therefore, the 301st would be red.

CHAPTER 2

Exponents and Roots

Rules of Operations with Exponents

To multiply two powers with the same base, keep the base and add the exponents together.

Example:

$2^2 \times 2^3 = (2 \times 2)(2 \times 2 \times 2) = 2^5$

or

$2^2 \times 2^3 = 2^{2+3} = 2^5$

To divide two powers with the same base, keep the base and subtract the exponent of the denominator from the exponent of the numerator.

Example:

$4^5 \div 4^2 = \dfrac{(4)(4)(4)(4)(4)}{(4)(4)} = 4^3$

or

$4^5 \div 4^2 = 4^{5-2} = 4^3$

To raise a power to another power, multiply the exponents.

Example:

$(3^2)^4 = (3 \times 3)^4$

or

$(3^2)^4 = (3 \times 3)(3 \times 3)(3 \times 3)(3 \times 3)$

or

$(3^2)^4 = 3^{2 \times 4} = 3^8$

NUMBER PROPERTIES

CHAPTER 2

Commonly Tested Properties of Powers

Many Data Sufficiency problems test your understanding of what happens when negative numbers and fractions are raised to a power.

Raising a fraction between zero and one to a power produces a smaller result.

Example:

$\left(\frac{1}{2}\right)^2 = \left(\frac{1}{2}\right)\left(\frac{1}{2}\right) = \frac{1}{4}$

Raising a negative number to an even power produces a positive result.

Example:

$(-2)^2 = 4$

Raising a negative number to an odd power gives a negative result.

Example:

$(-2)^3 = -8$

Powers of 10

When 10 is raised to an exponent that is a positive integer, that exponent tells how many zeros the number would contain if it were written out.

Example:

Write 10^6 in ordinary notation.

The exponent 6 indicates that you will need six zeros after the 1: 1,000,000. That's because 10^6 means six factors of 10, that is, (10)(10)(10)(10)(10)(10).

CHAPTER 2

To multiply a number by a power of 10, move the decimal point the same number of places to the right as the exponent (or as the number of zeros in that power of 10).

Example:

Multiply 0.029 by 10^3

The exponent is 3, so move the decimal point three places to the right.

$$(0.029)10^3 = 0029. = 29$$

If you had been told to multiply 0.029 by 1,000, you could have counted the number of zeros in 1,000 and done exactly the same thing.

Sometimes you'll have to add zeros as placeholders.

Example:

Multiply 0.029 by 10^6.

Add zeros until you can move the decimal point six places to the right:

$$0.029 \times 10^6 = 0029000. = 29,000$$

To divide by a power of 10, move the decimal point the corresponding number of places to the left, inserting zeros as placeholders if necessary.

Example:

Divide 416.03 by 10,000

There are four zeros in 10,000, but only three places to the left of the decimal point. You'll have to insert another zero:

$$416.03 \div 10,000 = .041603 = 0.041603$$

CHAPTER 2

By convention, one zero is usually written to the left of the decimal point on the GMAT. It's a placeholder and doesn't change the value of the number.

Scientific Notation

Very large numbers (and very small decimals) take up a lot of space and are difficult to work with. So in some scientific texts, they are expressed in a shorter, more convenient form, called scientific notation.

For example, 123,000,000,000 would be written in scientific notation as $(1.23)(10^{11})$, and 0.000000003 would be written as $(3.0)(10^{-9})$. (If you're already familiar with the concept of negative exponents, you'll know that multiplying by 10^{-9} is equivalent to dividing by 10^9.)

To express a number in scientific notation, rewrite it as a product of two factors. The first factor must be greater than or equal to 1 but less than 10. The second factor must be a power of 10.

To translate a number from scientific notation to ordinary notation, use the rules for multiplying and dividing by powers of 10.

Example:

$5.6 \times 10^6 = 5,600,000$, or 5.6 million

Rules of Operations with Roots and Radicals

A square root of any nonnegative number x is a number that, when multiplied by itself, yields x. Every positive number has two square roots, one positive and one negative. For instance, the positive square root of 25 is 5, because $5^2 = 25$. The negative square root of 25 is -5, because $(-5)^2$ also equals 25.

CHAPTER 2

By convention, the radical symbol $\sqrt{}$ stands for the positive square root only. Therefore, $\sqrt{9} = 3$ only, even though both 3^2 and $(-3)^2$ equal 9. This has important implications in Data Sufficiency.

Example:

What is the value of x?

(1) $x = \sqrt{16}$

(2) $x^2 = 16$

The first statement is sufficient, since there is only one possible value for $\sqrt{16}$, positive 4. The second statement is insufficient since x could be 4 or -4.

When applying the four basic arithmetic operations, radicals (roots written with the radical symbol) are treated in much the same way as variables.

Addition and Subtraction of Radicals

Only like radicals can be added to or subtracted from one another.

Example:

$2\sqrt{3} + 4\sqrt{2} - \sqrt{2} - 3\sqrt{3} =$

$(4\sqrt{2} - \sqrt{2}) + (2\sqrt{3} - 3\sqrt{3}) =$

$3\sqrt{2} + (-\sqrt{3}) =$

$3\sqrt{2} - \sqrt{3}$

This expression cannot be simplified any further.

CHAPTER 2

Multiplication and Division of Radicals

To multiply or divide one radical by another, multiply or divide the numbers outside the radical signs, then the numbers inside the radical signs.

Example:

$(6\sqrt{3})2\sqrt{5} = (6)(2)(\sqrt{3})(\sqrt{5}) = 12\sqrt{15}$

Example:

$12\sqrt{15} \div 2\sqrt{5} = \left(\dfrac{12}{2}\right)\left(\dfrac{\sqrt{15}}{\sqrt{5}}\right) = 6\sqrt{\dfrac{15}{5}} = 6\sqrt{3}$

Simplifying Radicals

If the number inside the radical is a multiple of a perfect square, the expression can be simplified by factoring out the perfect square.

Example:

$\sqrt{72} = (\sqrt{36})\sqrt{2} = 6\sqrt{2}$

CHAPTER 3

PROPORTIONS AND
MATH FORMULAS

CHAPTER

3

Fractions

The simplest way to understand the meaning of a fraction is to picture the denominator as the number of equal parts into which a whole unit is divided. The numerator represents a certain number of those equal parts.

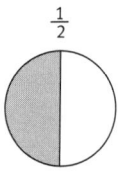 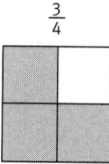

On the left, the shaded portion is one of two equal parts that make up the whole. On the right, the shaded portion is three of four equal parts that make up the whole.

The fraction bar is interchangeable with a division sign. You can divide the numerator of a fraction by the denominator to get an equivalent decimal. However, the numerator and denominator must each be treated as a single quantity.

Example:

Evaluate $\frac{5 + 2}{7 - 3}$

You can't just rewrite the fraction as $5 + 2 \div 7 - 3$, because the numerator and the denominator are each considered distinct quantities. Instead, you would rewrite the fraction as $(5 + 2) \div (7 - 3)$. The order of operations (remember PEMDAS?) tells us that operations in parentheses must be performed first. That gives you $7 \div 4$. Your final answer would be $\frac{7}{4}$, $1\frac{3}{4}$, or 1.75, depending on the form of the answer choices.

CHAPTER 3

Equivalent Fractions

Since multiplying or dividing a number by 1 does not change the number, multiplying the numerator and denominator of a fraction by the same nonzero number doesn't change the value of the fraction—it's the same as multiplying the entire fraction by 1.

Example:

Change $\frac{1}{2}$ into an equivalent fraction with a denominator of 4.

To change the denominator from 2 to 4, you'll have to multiply it by 2. But to keep the value of the fraction the same, you'll also have to multiply the numerator by 2.

$$\frac{1}{2} = \frac{1}{2}\left(\frac{2}{2}\right) = \frac{2}{4}$$

Similarly, dividing the numerator and denominator by the same nonzero number leaves the value of the fraction unchanged.

Example:

Change $\frac{16}{20}$ into an equivalent fraction with a denominator of 10.

To change the denominator from 20 to 10, you'll have to divide it by 2. But to keep the value of the fraction the same, you'll have to divide the numerator by the same number.

$$\frac{16}{20} = \frac{16 \div 2}{20 \div 2} = \frac{8}{10}$$

CHAPTER

3

Reducing (Canceling)

Most fractions on the GMAT are in lowest terms. That means that the numerator and denominator have no common factor greater than 1.

For example, the final answer of $\frac{8}{10}$ that we obtained in the previous example was not in lowest terms, because both 8 and 10 are divisible by 2. In contrast, the fraction $\frac{7}{10}$ is in lowest terms, because there is no factor greater than 1 that 7 and 10 have in common. To convert a fraction to its lowest terms, we use a method called reducing, or canceling. To reduce, simply divide any common factors out of both the numerator and the denominator.

Example:

Reduce $\frac{15}{35}$ to lowest terms.

$\frac{15}{35} = \frac{15 \div 5}{35 \div 5} = \frac{3}{7}$ (because a 5 cancels out, top and bottom)

The fastest way to reduce a fraction that has very large numbers in both the numerator and denominator is to find the greatest common factor and divide it out of both the top and the bottom.

Example:

Reduce $\frac{1040}{1080}$ to lowest terms.

$$\frac{1040}{1080} = \frac{104}{108} = \frac{52}{54} = \frac{26}{27}$$

CHAPTER 3

Adding and Subtracting Fractions

You cannot add or subtract fractions unless they have the same denominator. If they don't, you'll have to convert each fraction to an equivalent fraction with the least common denominator. Then add or subtract the numerators (not the denominators!) and, if necessary, reduce the resulting fraction to its lowest terms.

Given two fractions with different denominators, the least common denominator is the least common multiple of the two denominators, that is, the smallest number that is evenly divisible by both denominators.

Example:

What is the least common denominator of $\frac{2}{15}$ and $\frac{3}{10}$?

The least common denominator of the two fractions will be the least common multiple of 15 and 10.

Because $15 = (5)(3)$ and $10 = (5)(2)$, the least common multiple of the two numbers is $(5)(3)(2)$, or 30. That makes 30 the least common denominator of $\frac{2}{15}$ and $\frac{3}{10}$.

Example:

$\frac{2}{15} + \frac{3}{10} = ?$

As we saw in the previous example, the least common denominator of the two fractions is 30. Change each fraction to an equivalent fraction with a denominator of 30.

$$\frac{2}{15}\left(\frac{2}{2}\right) = \frac{4}{30}$$
$$\frac{3}{10}\left(\frac{3}{3}\right) = \frac{9}{30}$$

PROPORTIONS AND MATH FORMULAS

CHAPTER 3

Then add:

$$\frac{4}{30} + \frac{9}{30} = \frac{13}{30}$$

Since 13 and 30 have no common factor greater than 1, $\frac{13}{30}$ is in lowest terms. You can't reduce it further.

Multiplying Fractions

To multiply fractions, multiply the numerators and multiply the denominators.

$$\frac{5}{7}\left(\frac{3}{4}\right) = \frac{15}{28}$$

Multiplying numerator by numerator and denominator by denominator is simple. But it's easy to make careless errors if you have to multiply a string of fractions or work with large numbers. You can minimize those errors by reducing before you multiply.

Example:

Multiply $\left(\frac{10}{9}\right)\left(\frac{3}{4}\right)\left(\frac{8}{15}\right)$.

First, cancel a 5 out of the 10 and the 15, a 3 out of the 3 and the 9, and a 4 out of the 8 and the 4:

$$\left(\frac{\cancel{10}^{2}}{\cancel{9}_{3}}\right)\left(\frac{\cancel{3}^{1}}{\cancel{4}_{1}}\right)\left(\frac{\cancel{8}^{2}}{\cancel{15}_{3}}\right)$$

Then multiply numerators together and denominators together:

$$\left(\frac{2}{3}\right)\left(\frac{1}{1}\right)\left(\frac{2}{3}\right) = \frac{4}{9}$$

CHAPTER 3

Reciprocals

To get the reciprocal of a common fraction, turn the fraction upside-down so that the numerator becomes the denominator, and vice versa. If a fraction has a numerator of 1, the fraction's reciprocal will be equivalent to an integer.

Example:

What is the reciprocal of $\frac{1}{25}$?

Inverting the fraction gives you the reciprocal, $\frac{25}{1}$. But dividing a number by 1 doesn't change the value of the number.

Since $\frac{25}{1} = 25$, the reciprocal of $\frac{1}{25}$ equals 25.

Dividing Common Fractions

To divide fractions, multiply by the reciprocal of the number or fraction that follows the division sign.

$$\frac{1}{2} \div \frac{3}{5} = \frac{1}{2}\left(\frac{5}{3}\right) = \frac{5}{6}$$

(The operation of division produces the same result as multiplication by the inverse.)

Example:

$$\frac{4}{3} \div \frac{4}{9} = \frac{4}{3}\left(\frac{9}{4}\right) = \frac{36}{12} = 3$$

PROPORTIONS AND MATH FORMULAS

CHAPTER 3

Comparing Positive Fractions

Given two positive fractions with the same denominator, the fraction with the larger numerator will have the larger value.

Example:

Which is greater, $\frac{3}{8}$ or $\frac{5}{8}$?

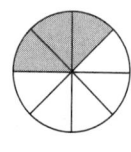

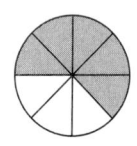

$$\frac{3}{8} < \frac{5}{8}$$

But if you're given two positive fractions with the same numerator but different denominators, the fraction with the smaller denominator will have the larger value.

Example:

Which is greater, $\frac{3}{4}$ or $\frac{3}{8}$?

The diagrams below show two wholes of equal size. The one on the left is divided into 4 equal parts, 3 of which are shaded. The one on the right is divided into 8 equal parts, 3 of which are shaded.

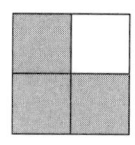

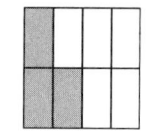

$\frac{3}{4}$ is clearly greater than $\frac{3}{8}$

CHAPTER 3

If neither the numerators nor the denominators are the same, you have three options. You can turn both fractions into their decimal equivalents. Or you can express both fractions in terms of some common denominator and then see which new equivalent fraction has the largest numerator. Or you can cross multiply the numerator of each fraction by the denominator of the other. The greater result will wind up next to the greater fraction.

Example:

Which is greater, $\frac{5}{6}$ or $\frac{7}{9}$?

$$45 \quad\quad 42$$
$$\frac{5}{6} \times \frac{7}{9}$$

Since $45 > 42$, $\frac{5}{6} > \frac{7}{9}$.

Mixed Numbers and Improper Fractions

A *mixed number* consists of an integer and a fraction.

An improper fraction is a fraction whose numerator is greater than its denominator. To convert an improper fraction to a mixed number, divide the numerator by the denominator. The number of "whole" times that the denominator goes into the numerator will be the integer portion of the improper fraction; the remainder will be the numerator of the fractional portion.

Example:

Convert $\frac{23}{4}$ to a mixed number.

Dividing 23 by 4 gives you 5 with a remainder of 3, so $\frac{23}{4} = 5\frac{3}{4}$.

CHAPTER 3

To change a mixed number to a fraction, multiply the integer portion of the mixed number by the denominator and add the numerator. This new number is your numerator. The denominator will not change.

Example:

Convert $2\frac{3}{7}$ to a fraction.

$$2\frac{3}{7} = \frac{7(2) + 3}{7} = \frac{17}{7}$$

Properties of Fractions Between −1 and +1

The reciprocal of a fraction between 0 and 1 is greater than both the original fraction and 1.

Example:

The reciprocal of $\frac{2}{3}$ is $\frac{3}{2}$, which is greater than both 1 and $\frac{2}{3}$.

The reciprocal of a fraction between −1 and 0 is less than both the original fraction and −1.

Example:

The reciprocal of $-\frac{2}{3}$ is $-\frac{3}{2}$, or $-1\frac{1}{2}$, which is less than both −1 and $-\frac{2}{3}$.

CHAPTER 3

The square of a fraction between 0 and 1 is less than the original fraction.

Example:

$\left(\frac{1}{2}\right)^2 = \left(\frac{1}{2}\right)\left(\frac{1}{2}\right) = \frac{1}{4}$

But the square of any fraction between 0 and −1 is greater than the original fraction, because multiplying two negative numbers gives you a positive product, and any positive number is greater than any negative number.

Example:

$\left(-\frac{1}{2}\right)^2 = \left(-\frac{1}{2}\right)\left(-\frac{1}{2}\right) = \frac{1}{4}$

Multiplying any positive number by a fraction between 0 and 1 gives a product smaller than the original number.

Example:

$6\left(\frac{1}{4}\right) = \frac{6}{4} = \frac{3}{2}$

Multiplying any negative number by a fraction between 0 and 1 gives a product greater than the original number.

Example:

$(-3)\left(\frac{1}{2}\right) = -\frac{3}{2}$

PROPORTIONS AND MATH FORMULAS

CHAPTER 3

Decimals

Converting Decimals

It's easy to convert decimals to common fractions, and vice versa. Any decimal fraction is equivalent to some common fraction with a power of 10 in the denominator.

To convert a decimal between 0 and 1 to a fraction, determine the place value of the last nonzero digit and set this as the denominator. Then use all the digits of the decimal number as the numerator, ignoring the decimal point. Finally, if necessary, reduce the fraction to its lowest terms.

Example:

Convert 0.875 to a fraction in lowest terms.

The last nonzero digit is the 5, which is in the thousandths place. So the denominator of the common fraction will be 1,000. The numerator will be 875: $\frac{875}{1000}$.

(You can ignore the zero to the left of the decimal point, since there are no nonzero digits to its left; it's just a "placeholder.")

Both 875 and 1,000 contain a factor of 25. Canceling it out leaves you with $\frac{35}{40}$. Reducing that further by a factor of 5 gives you $\frac{7}{8}$, which is in lowest terms.

CHAPTER 3

To convert a fraction to a decimal, simply divide the numerator by the denominator.

Example:

What is the decimal equivalent of $\frac{4}{5}$?

$$4 \div 5 = 0.8$$

Comparing Decimals

Knowing place values allows you to assess the relative values of decimals.

Example:

Which is greater, 0.254 or 0.3?

Of course, 254 is greater than 3. But $0.3 = \frac{3}{10}$, which is equivalent to $\frac{300}{1000}$, while 0.254 is equivalent to only $\frac{254}{1000}$. Since $\frac{300}{1000} > \frac{254}{1000}$, 0.3 is greater than 0.254.

Here's the simplest way to compare decimals: Add zeros after the last digit to the right of the decimal point in each decimal fraction until all the decimals you're comparing have the same number of digits. Essentially, what you're doing is giving all the fractions the same denominator so that you can just compare their numerators.

CHAPTER 3

Example:

Arrange in order from smallest to largest: 0.7, 0.77, 0.07, 0.707, and 0.077.

The numbers 0.707 and 0.077 end at the third place to the right of the decimal point—the thousandths place. Add zeros after the last digit to the right of the decimal point in each of the other fractions until you reach the thousandths place:

$$0.7 = 0.700 = \frac{700}{1000}$$

$$0.77 = 0.770 = \frac{770}{1000}$$

$$0.07 = 0.070 = \frac{70}{1000}$$

$$0.707 = \frac{707}{1000}$$

$$0.077 = \frac{77}{1000}$$

$$\frac{70}{1000} < \frac{77}{1000} < \frac{700}{1000} < \frac{707}{1000} < \frac{770}{1000}$$

Therefore, $0.07 < 0.077 < 0.7 < 0.707 < 0.77$.

CHAPTER

3

Estimation and Rounding on the GMAT

You should be familiar and comfortable with the practice of "rounding off" numbers. To round off a number to a particular place, look at the digit immediately to the right of that place. If the digit is 0, 1, 2, 3, or 4, don't change the digit that is in the place to which you are rounding. If it is 5, 6, 7, 8, or 9, change the digit in the place to which you are rounding to the next higher digit. Replace all digits to the right of the place to which you are rounding with zeros.

For example, to round off 235 to the tens place, look at the units place. Since it is occupied by a 5, you'll round the 3 in the tens place up to a 4, giving you 240. If you had been rounding off 234, you would have rounded down to the existing 3 in the tens place; that would have given you 230.

Example:

Round off 675,978 to the hundreds place.

The 7 in the tens place means that you will have to round the hundreds place up. Since there is a 9 in the hundreds place, you'll have to change the thousands place as well. Rounding 675,978 to the hundreds place gives you 676,000.

Rounding off large numbers before calculation will allow you quickly to estimate the correct answer.

Estimating can save you valuable time on many GMAT problems. But before you estimate, check the answer choices to see how close they are. If they are relatively close together, you'll have to be more accurate than if they are farther apart.

CHAPTER

3

Percents

The word *percent* means "hundredths," and the percent sign, %, means $\frac{1}{100}$. For example, 25% means $25\left(\frac{1}{100}\right) = \frac{25}{100}$. (Like the division sign, the percent sign evolved from the fractional relationship; the slanted bar in a percent sign represents a fraction bar.)

Percents measure a part-to-whole relationship with an assumed whole equal to 100. The percent relationship can be expressed as $\frac{Part}{Whole}$ (100%). For example, if $\frac{1}{4}$ of a rectangle is shaded, the percent of the rectangle that is shaded is $\frac{1}{4}$ (100%) = 25%.

Like fractions, percents express the relationship between a specified part and a whole. In fact, by plugging the part and whole from the shaded rectangle problem into the fraction and decimal versions of the part-whole equation, you can verify that 25%, $\frac{25}{100}$, and 0.25 are simply different names for the same part-whole relationship.

Translating English to Math in Part-Whole Problems

On the GMAT, many fractions and percents appear in word problems. You'll solve the problems by plugging the numbers you're given into some variation of one of the three basic formulas:

$$\frac{Part}{Whole} = Fraction$$

$$\frac{Part}{Whole} = Decimal$$

$$\frac{Part}{Whole}(100) = Percent$$

CHAPTER 3

To avoid careless errors, look for the key words *is* and *of*. *Is* (or *are*) often introduces the part, while *of* almost invariably introduces the whole.

Properties of 100%

Since the percent sign means $\frac{1}{100}$, 100% means $\frac{100}{100}$, or one whole. The key to solving some GMAT percent problems is to recognize that all the parts add up to one whole: 100%.

Example:

All 1,000 registered voters in Smithtown are Democrats, Republicans, or independents. If 75% of the registered voters are Democrats, and 5% are independents, how many are Republicans?

We calculate that 75% + 5%, or 80% of the 1,000 registered voters are either Democrats or independents. The three party affiliations together must account for 100% of the voters; thus, the percentage of Republicans must be 100% − 80%, or 20%. Therefore, the number of Republicans must be 20% of 1,000, which is 20% (1,000), or 200.

Multiplying or dividing a number by 100% is just like multiplying or dividing by 1; it doesn't change the value of the original number.

PROPORTIONS AND MATH FORMULAS

CHAPTER 3

Converting Percents

To change a fraction to its percent equivalent, multiply by 100%.

Example:

What is the percent equivalent of $\frac{5}{8}$?

$$\frac{5}{8}(100\%) = \frac{500}{8}\% = 62\frac{1}{2}\%$$

To change a decimal fraction to a percent, you can use the rules for multiplying by powers of 10. Move the decimal point two places to the right and insert a percent sign.

Example:

What is the percent equivalent of 0.17?

$$0.17 = 0.17(100\%) = 17\%$$

To change a percent to its fractional equivalent, divide by 100%.

Example:

What is the common fraction equivalent of 32%?

$$32\% = \frac{32\%}{100\%} = \frac{8}{25}$$

To convert a percent to its decimal equivalent, use the rules for dividing by powers of 10—just move the decimal point two places to the left.

Example:

What is the decimal equivalent of 32%?

$$32\% = \frac{32\%}{100\%} = \frac{32}{100} = 0.32$$

CHAPTER 3

When you divide a percent by another percent, the percent sign "drops out," just as you would cancel out a common factor.

Example:

$$\frac{100\%}{5\%} = \frac{100}{5} = 20$$

Translation: There are 20 groups of 5% in 100%.

But when you divide a percent by a regular number (not by another percent), the percent sign remains.

Example:

$$\frac{100\%}{5} = 20\%$$

Translation: One-fifth of 100% is 20%.

CHAPTER 3

Common Percent Equivalents

As you can see, changing percents to fractions, or vice versa, is pretty straightforward. But it does take a second or two that you might spend more profitably doing other computations or setting up another GMAT math problem. Familiarity with the following common equivalents will save you time.

$$\frac{1}{20} = 5\% \qquad \frac{1}{2} = 50\%$$

$$\frac{1}{12} = 8\frac{1}{3}\% \qquad \frac{3}{5} = 60\%$$

$$\frac{1}{10} = 10\% \qquad \frac{5}{8} = 62\frac{1}{2}\%$$

$$\frac{1}{8} = 12\frac{1}{2}\% \qquad \frac{2}{3} = 66\frac{2}{3}\%$$

$$\frac{1}{6} = 16\frac{2}{3}\% \qquad \frac{7}{10} = 70\%$$

$$\frac{1}{5} = 20\% \qquad \frac{3}{4} = 75\%$$

$$\frac{1}{4} = 25\% \qquad \frac{4}{5} = 80\%$$

$$\frac{3}{10} = 30\% \qquad \frac{5}{6} = 83\frac{1}{3}\%$$

$$\frac{1}{3} = 33\frac{1}{3}\% \qquad \frac{7}{8} = 87\frac{1}{2}\%$$

$$\frac{3}{8} = 37\frac{1}{2}\% \qquad \frac{9}{10} = 90\%$$

$$\frac{2}{5} = 40\% \qquad \frac{11}{12} = 91\frac{2}{3}\%$$

CHAPTER

3

Using the Percent Formula to Solve Percent Problems

You can solve most percent problems by plugging the given data into the percent formula:

$$\frac{\text{part}}{\text{Whole}}(100\%) = \text{Percent}$$

Most percent problems give you two of the three variables and ask for the third.

Example:

Ben spends $30 of his annual gardening budget on seed. If his total annual gardening budget is $150, what percentage of his budget does he spend on seed?

This problem specifies the whole ($150) and the part ($30) and asks for the percentage. Plugging those numbers into the percent formula gives you this:

$$\text{Percent} = \frac{30}{150}(100\%) = \frac{1}{5}(100\%) = 20$$

Ben spends 20% of his annual gardening budget on seed.

Percent Increase and Decrease

When the GMAT tests percent increase or decrease, use the formulas:

$$\text{Percent increase} = \frac{\text{Increase }(100\%)}{\text{Original}} \text{ or Percent decrease} = \frac{\text{Decrease }(100\%)}{\text{Original}}.$$

To find the increase or decrease, just take the difference between the original and the new. Note that the "original" is the base from which change occurs. It may or may not be the first number mentioned in the problem.

PROPORTIONS AND MATH FORMULAS

CHAPTER 3

Example:

Two years ago, 450 seniors graduated from Inman High School. Last year, 600 seniors graduated. By what percentage did the number of graduating seniors increase?

The original is the figure from the earlier time (two years ago): 450. The increase is 600 − 450, or 150. So the percentage increase is $\frac{150}{450}(100\%) = 33\frac{1}{3}\%$.

Example:

If the price of a $120 dress is increased by 25%, what is the new selling price?

To find the new whole, you'll first have to find the amount of increase. The original whole is $120, and the percent increase is 25%. Plugging in, we find that

$$\frac{\text{increase}}{120}(100\%) = 25\%$$

$$\frac{\text{increase}}{120} = \frac{25}{100}$$

$$\frac{\text{increase}}{120} = \frac{1}{4}$$

$$\text{increase} = \frac{120}{4}$$

$$\text{increase} = 30$$

The amount of increase is $30, so the new selling price is $120 + $30, or $150.

CHAPTER 3

Multistep Percent Problems

On some difficult problems, you'll be asked to find more than one percent, or to find a percent of a percent. Be careful: You can't add percents of different wholes.

Example:

The price of an antique is reduced by 20 percent, and then this price is reduced by 10 percent. If the antique originally cost $200, what is its final price?

The most common mistake in this kind of problem is to reduce the original price by a total of 20% + 10%, or 30%. That would make the final price 70 percent of the original, or 70% ($200) = $140. This is not the correct answer. In this example, the second (10%) price reduction is taken off of the first sale price—the new whole, not the original whole.

To get the correct answer, first find the new whole. You can find it by calculating either $200 − (20% of $200) or 80% ($200). Either way, you will find that the first sale price is $160. That price then has to be reduced by 10%. Either calculate $160 − (10% ($160)) or 90%($160). In either case, the final price of the antique is $144.

Picking Numbers with Percents

Certain types of percent problems lend themselves readily to the alternative technique of Picking Numbers. These include problems in which no actual values are mentioned, just percents. If you assign values to the percents you are working with, you'll find the problem less abstract.

You should almost always pick 100 in percent problems, because it's relatively easy to find percentages of 100.

CHAPTER 3

Example:

The price of a share of company A's stock fell by 20 percent two weeks ago and by another 25 percent last week to its current price. By what percent of the current price does the share price need to rise in order to return to its original price?

- ○ 45%
- ○ 55%
- ○ $66\frac{2}{3}$%
- ○ 75%
- ○ 82%

Pick a value for the original price of the stock. Since it is a percent question, picking $100 will make the math easy. The first change in the price of the stock was by 20% of $100, or $20, making the new price $100 − $20 = $80. The price then fell by another 25%.

25% is the same as $\frac{1}{4}$, and $\frac{1}{4}$ of $80 is $20. Therefore, the current price is $80 − $20 = $60. To return to its original price, the stock needs to rise from $60 to $100, that is, by $100 − $60 = $40. Then $40 is what percent of the current price, $60?

$$\frac{40}{60}(100\%) = \frac{2}{3}(100\%) = 66\frac{2}{3}\%$$

CHAPTER 3

Percent Word Problems

Percent problems are often presented as word problems. We have already seen how to identify the percent, the part, and the whole in simple percent word problems. Here are some other terms that you are likely to encounter in more complicated percent word problems:

Profit made on an item is the seller's price minus the costs to the seller. If a seller buys an item for $10 and sells it for $12, he or she has made $2 profit. The percent of the selling price that is profit is $\frac{\text{Profit}}{\text{Original selling price}} (100\%) = \frac{\$2}{\$12} (100\%) = 16\frac{2}{3}\%$.

A *discount* on an item is the original price minus the reduced price. If an item that usually sells for $20 is sold for $15, the discount is $5. Discount is often represented as a percentage of the original price. In this case, the percentage discount $= \frac{\text{Discount}}{\text{Original price}} (100\%) = \frac{\$5}{\$20} = 25\%$.

The *sale price* is the final price after discount or decrease.

Occasionally, percent problems will involve *interest*. Interest is given as a percent per unit time, such as 5% per month. The sum of money invested is the *principal*. The most common type of interest you will see is *simple interest*. In simple interest, the interest payments received are kept separate from the principal.

Example:

If an investor invests $100 at 20 percent simple annual interest, how much does he or she have at the end of 3 years?

The principal of $100 yields 20% interest every year. Because 20% of $100 is $20, after three years the investor will have 3 years of interest, or $60, plus the principal, for a total of $160.

CHAPTER 3

In *compound interest*, the money earned as interest is reinvested. The principal grows after every interest payment received.

Example:

If an investor invests $100 at 20% compounded annually, how much does he or she have at the end of 3 years?

The first year the investor earns 20% of $100 = $20. So, after one year he or she has $100 + $20 = $120.

The second year the investor earns 20% of $120 = $24. So, after two years he or she has $120 + $24 = $144.

The third year the investor earns 20% of $144 = $28.80. So, after 3 years he or she has $144 + $28.80 = $172.80.

Percents and Data Sufficiency

Data Sufficiency questions (covered in Session 2) test your knowledge of percents in a different way. The crux of these problems, as a rule, is finding all the pieces of the percent formula. You can use the percent formula to pinpoint exactly what you need to achieve sufficiency.

Example:

By what percent did the price of stock X increase?

(1) The price after the increase was $12.

(2) The stock increased in price by $1.50.

To prove sufficiency, you would have to be capable of filling in all parts of the equation. Statement (1) informs you of the price after the increase. This does not give you either the amount of increase or the original price, so it is not sufficient. Statement (2) informs you of the increase in price, but not the original price, so it, too, is not sufficient. Combining the statements, however, gives you the increase in price, $1.50, and the original price, $12.00 − $1.50 = $10.50. So the correct answer is choice **(C)**.

CHAPTER

3

Ratios

A ratio is the proportional relationship between two quantities. The ratio, or relationship, between two numbers, for example, 10 and 15, may be expressed with a colon between the two numbers (10:15), in words ("the ratio of 10 to 15"), or as a common fraction $\left(\frac{10}{15}\right)$.

To translate a ratio in words to numbers separated by a colon, replace *to* with a colon.

To translate a ratio in words to a fractional ratio, use whatever follows the word *of* as the numerator and whatever follows the word *to* as the denominator. For example, if we had to express the ratio of glazed doughnuts *to* chocolate doughnuts in a box of doughnuts that contained 5 glazed and 7 chocolate doughnuts, we would do so as $\frac{5}{7}$.

Note that the fraction $\frac{5}{7}$ does not mean that $\frac{5}{7}$ of all the doughnuts are glazed doughnuts. There are 5 + 7, or 12 doughnuts all together, so of the doughnuts, $\frac{5}{12}$ are glazed. The $\frac{5}{7}$ ratio merely indicates the proportion of glazed to chocolate doughnuts. For every five glazed doughnuts, there are seven chocolate doughnuts.

Treating ratios as fractions usually makes computation easier. Like fractions, ratios often require division. And, like fractions, ratios can be reduced to lowest terms.

Example:

Joe is 16 years old, and Mary is 12 years old. Express the ratio of Joe's age to Mary's age in lowest terms.

The ratio of Joe's age to Mary's age is $\frac{16}{12} = \frac{4}{3}$, or 4:3.

CHAPTER 3

Part:Whole Ratios

In a part:whole ratio, the "whole" is the entire set (for instance, all the workers in a factory), while the "part" is a certain subset of the whole (for instance, all the female workers in the factory).

In GMAT ratio question stems, the word *fraction* generally indicates a part:whole ratio. "What fraction of the workers are female?" means "What is the ratio of the number of female workers to the total number of workers?"

Example:

The sophomore class at Milford Academy consists of 15 boys and 20 girls. What fraction of the sophomore class is female?

The following three statements are equivalent:

1. $\frac{4}{7}$ of the sophomores are female.

2. 4 out of every 7 sophomores are female.

3. The ratio of female sophomores to total sophomores is 4:7.

Ratio vs. Actual Number

Ratios are usually reduced to their simplest form (that is, to lowest terms). If the ratio of men to women in a room is 5:3, you cannot necessarily infer that there are exactly five men and three women.

If you knew the total number of people in the room, in addition to the male to female ratio, you could determine the number of men and the number of women in the room. For example, suppose you know that there are 32 people in the room. If the male to female ratio is 5 to 3, then the ratio of males to the total is 5:(5 + 3), which is 5:8. You can set

CHAPTER 3

up an equation as $\frac{5}{8} = \frac{\text{\# of males in room}}{32}$. Solving, you will find that the number of males in the room is 20.

Example:

The ratio of domestic sales revenues to foreign sales revenues of a certain product is 3:5. What fraction of the total sales revenues comes from domestic sales?

At first, this question may look more complicated than the previous example. You have to convert from a part:part ratio to a part:whole ratio (the ratio of domestic sales revenues to total sales revenues). And you're not given actual dollar figures for domestic or foreign sales. But since all sales are either foreign or domestic, "total sales revenues" must be the sum of the revenues from domestic and foreign sales. You can convert the given ratio to a part:whole ratio, because the sum of the parts equals the whole.

Although it's impossible to determine dollar amounts for the domestic, foreign, or total sales revenues from the given information, the 3:5 ratio tells you that of every $8 in sales revenues, $3 come from domestic sales and $5 from foreign sales. Therefore, the ratio of domestic sales revenues to total sales revenues is 3:8, or $\frac{3}{8}$.

You can convert a part:part ratio to a part:whole ratio (or vice versa) only if there are no missing parts and no overlap among the parts; that is, if the whole is equal to the sum of the parts.

PROPORTIONS AND MATH FORMULAS

CHAPTER 3

This concept is often tested in Data Sufficiency.

Example:

In a certain bag, what is the ratio of the number of red marbles to the total number of marbles?

(1) The ratio of the number of red marbles to the number of blue marbles in the bag is 3:5.

(2) There are only red and blue marbles in the bag.

In this case, Statement (1), by itself, is insufficient. You cannot convert a part-to-part ratio (red marbles to blue marbles) to a part-to-whole ratio (red marbles to all marbles) because you don't know whether there were any other colored marbles in the bag. Only when you combine the two statements do you have enough information to answer the question, so the answer is **(C)**.

Example:

Of the 25 people in Fran's apartment building, what is the ratio of people who use the roof to total residents?

(1) There are 9 residents who use the roof for tanning and 8 residents who use the roof for gardening.

(2) The roof is only used by tanners and gardeners.

In this question, we do not know if there is any overlap between tanners and gardeners. How many, if any, residents do both? Since we don't know, the answer is **(E)**.

CHAPTER

3

Ratios of More Than Two Terms

Most of the ratios that you'll see on the GMAT have two terms. But it is possible to set up ratios with more than two terms. These ratios express more relationships, and therefore convey more information, than two-term ratios. However, most of the principles discussed so far with respect to two-term ratios are just as applicable to ratios of more than two terms.

Example:

The ratio of x to y is 5:4. The ratio of y to z is 1:2. What is the ratio of x to z?

We want the y's in the two ratios to equal each other, because then we can combine the x:y ratio and the y:z ratio to form the x:y:z ratio that we need to answer this question. To make the y's equal, we can multiply the second ratio by 4. When we do so, we must perform the multiplication on both components of the ratio. Since a ratio is a constant proportion, it can be multiplied or divided by any number without losing its meaning, as long as the multiplication and division are applied to all the components of the ratio. In this case, we find that the new ratio for y to z is 4:8. We can combine this with the first ratio to find a new x to y to z ratio of 5:4:8. Therefore, the ratio of x to z is 5:8.

CHAPTER

3

Rates

A rate is a special type of ratio. Instead of relating a part to the whole, or to another part, a rate relates one kind of quantity to a completely different kind. When we talk about rates, we usually use the word *per*, as in "miles per hour," "cost per item," etc. Since *per* means "for one" or "for each," we express the rates as ratios reduced to a denominator of 1.

Speed

The most commonly tested rate on the GMAT is speed. This is usually expressed in miles or kilometers per hour. The relationship between speed, distance, and time is given by the formula Speed = $\frac{\text{Distance}}{\text{Time}}$ which can be rewritten two ways: Time = $\frac{\text{Distance}}{\text{Speed}}$, and Distance = (Speed)(Time).

Any time you can find two out of the three elements in this equation, you can find the third.

For example, if a car travels 300 miles in 5 hours, it has averaged $\frac{300 \text{ miles}}{5 \text{ hours}}$ = 60 miles per hour. (Note that speeds are usually expressed as averages because they are not necessarily constant. For instance, in the previous example, the car traveled 300 miles in 5 hours. It moved at an "average speed" of 60 miles per hour, but probably not at a constant speed of 60 miles per hour.)

Likewise, a rearranged version of the formula can be used to solve for missing speed or time.

CHAPTER 3

Example:

How far do you drive if you travel for 5 hours at 60 miles per hour?

$$\text{Distance} = (\text{Speed})(\text{Time})$$
$$\text{Distance} = (60 \text{ mph})(5 \text{ hours})$$
$$\text{Distance} = 300 \text{ miles}$$

Example:

How much time does it take to drive 300 miles at 60 miles per hour?

$$\text{Time} = \frac{\text{Distance}}{\text{Speed}}$$
$$\text{Time} = \frac{300 \text{ miles}}{60 \text{ mph}}$$
$$\text{Time} = 5 \text{ hours}$$

Other Rates

Speed is not the only rate that appears on the GMAT. For instance, you might get a word problem involving liters per minute or cost per unit. All rate problems, however, can be solved using the speed formula and its variants by conceiving of "speed" as "rate," and "distance" as "quantity."

Example:

How many hours will it take to fill a 500-liter tank at a rate of 2 liters per minute?

Plug the numbers into our rate formula:

$$\text{Time} = \frac{\text{Quantity}}{\text{Rate}}$$
$$\text{Time} = \frac{500 \text{ liters}}{2 \text{ liters per minute}}$$
$$\text{Time} = 250 \text{ minutes}$$

Now convert 250 minutes to hours: 250 minutes ÷ 60 minutes per hour = $4\frac{1}{6}$ hours to fill the pool. (As you can see from this problem, GMAT Problem Solving questions test your ability to convert minutes into hours and vice versa. Pay close attention to what units the answer choice must use.)

In some cases, you should use proportions to answer rate questions.

Example:

If 350 widgets cost $20, how much will 1,400 widgets cost at the same rate?

Set up a proportion:

$$\frac{\text{Number of widgets}}{\text{Cost}} = \frac{350 \text{ widgets}}{\$20} = \frac{1400 \text{ widgets}}{\$x}$$

Solving, you will find that $x = 80$.

So, 1,400 widgets will cost $80 at that rate.

Combined Rate Problems

Rates can be added.

Example:

Nelson can mow 200 square meters of lawn per hour. John can mow 100 square meters of lawn per hour. Working simultaneously but independently, how many hours will it take Nelson and John to mow 1,800 square meters of lawn?

Add Nelson's rate to John's rate to find the combined rate.

CHAPTER 3

200 meters per hour + 100 meters per hour = 300 meters per hour.

Divide the total lawn area, 1,800 square meters, by the combined rate, 300 square meters per hour, to find the number of required hours, 6.

Work Problems (Given Hours per Unit of Work)

The work formula can be used to find out how long it takes a number of people working together to complete a task. Let's say we have three people. The first takes a units of time to complete the job, the second b units of time to complete the job, and the third c units of time. If the time it takes all three working together to complete the job is T, then $\frac{1}{a} + \frac{1}{b} + \frac{1}{c} = \frac{1}{T}$.

Example:

John can weed the garden in 3 hours. If Mary can weed the garden in 2 hours, how long will it take them to weed the garden at this rate, working independently?

Set John's time per unit of work as a and Mary's time per unit of work as b. (There is no need for the variable c, since there are only two people.) Plugging in, you find that

$$\frac{1}{3} + \frac{1}{2} = \frac{1}{T}$$

$$\frac{2}{6} + \frac{3}{6} = \frac{1}{T}$$

$$\frac{5}{6} = \frac{1}{T}$$

$$T = \frac{6}{5} \text{ hours}$$

PROPORTIONS AND MATH FORMULAS

CHAPTER 3

Work Formula

We can use the above equation, $\frac{1}{a} + \frac{1}{b} = \frac{1}{T}$, to derive the work formula, a convenient formula to use on Test Day.

$$\frac{1}{a} + \frac{1}{b} = \frac{1}{T}$$

$$(ab)\left(\frac{1}{a} + \frac{1}{b}\right) = \left(\frac{1}{T}\right)(ab)$$

$$\frac{ab}{a} + \frac{ab}{b} = \frac{ab}{T}$$

$$b + a = \frac{ab}{T}$$

$$T(b + a) = \left(\frac{ab}{T}\right)T$$

$$T(b + a) = ab$$

$$T = \frac{ab}{a + b}$$

This last equation is the work formula.

Here, $a =$ the amount of time is takes person a to complete the job and $b =$ the amount of time it takes person b to complete the job.

Example:

Let's use the same example from above: John takes 3 hours to weed the garden, and Mary takes 2 hours to weed the same garden. How long will it take them to weed the garden together?

Work formula $= \frac{a \times b}{a + b} = \frac{3 \times 2}{3 + 2} = \frac{6}{5}$ hours

CHAPTER 3

Averages

The average of a group of numbers is defined as the sum of the terms divided by the number of terms.

$$\text{Average} = \frac{\text{Sum of terms}}{\text{Number of terms}}$$

This equation can be rewritten two ways:

$$\text{Number of terms} = \frac{\text{Sum of terms}}{\text{Average}}$$

$$\text{Sum of terms} = (\text{Number of terms})(\text{Average})$$

Thus, any time you have two out of the three values (average, sum of terms, number of terms), you can find the third.

Example:

Henry buys three items costing $2.00, $1.75, and $1.05. What is the average price (arithmetic mean) of the three items? (Don't let the phrase *arithmetic mean* throw you; it's just another term for *average*.)

$$\text{Average} = \frac{\text{Sum of terms}}{\text{Number of terms}}$$

$$\text{Average} = \frac{\$2.0 + \$1.75 + \$1.05}{3}$$

$$\text{Average} = \frac{\$4.80}{3}$$

$$\text{Average} = \$1.60$$

CHAPTER 3

Example:

June pays an average price of $14.50 for 6 articles of clothing. What is the total price of all 6 articles?

$$\text{Sum of terms} = (\text{Average})(\text{Number of terms})$$

$$\text{Sum of terms} = (\$14.50)(6)$$

$$\text{Sum of terms} = \$87.00$$

Example:

The total weight of the licorice sticks in a jar is 30 ounces. If the average weight of each licorice stick is 2 ounces, how many licorice sticks are there in the jar?

$$\text{Number of terms} = \frac{\text{Sum of terms}}{\text{Average}}$$

$$\text{Number of terms} = \frac{30 \text{ ounces}}{2 \text{ ounces}}$$

$$\text{Number of terms} = 15$$

Using the Average to Find a Missing Number

If you're given the average, the total number of terms, and all but one of the actual numbers, you can find the missing number.

Example:

The average annual rainfall in Boynton for 1976–1979 was 26 inches per year. Boynton received 24 inches of rain in 1976, 30 inches in 1977, and 19 inches in 1978. How many inches of rainfall did Boynton receive in 1979?

You know that total rainfall equals 24 + 30 + 19 + (number of inches of rain in 1979).

You know that the average rainfall was 26 inches per year.

You know that there were 4 years.

So, plug these numbers into any of the three expressions of the average formula to find that Sum of terms = (Average)(Number of terms)

$$24 + 30 + 19 + \text{inches in 1979} = (26)(4)$$
$$73 + \text{inches in 1979} = (26)(4)$$
$$73 + \text{inches in 1979} = 104$$
$$\text{inches in 1979} = 31$$

Another Way to Find a Missing Number: The Concept of "Balanced Value"

Another way to find a missing number is to understand that the *sum of the differences between each term and the mean of the set must equal zero*. Plugging in the numbers from the previous problem, for example, we find that

$$(24 - 26) + (30 - 26) + (19 - 26) + (\text{inches in 1979} - 26) = 0$$
$$(-2) + (4) + (-7) + (\text{inches in 1979} - 26) = 0$$
$$-5 + (\text{inches in 1979} - 26) = 0$$
$$\text{inches in 1979} = 31$$

It may be easier to comprehend why this is true by visualizing a balancing, or weighting, process. The combined distance of the numbers above the average from the mean must be balanced with the combined distance of the numbers below the average from the mean.

CHAPTER 3

Example:

The average of 63, 64, 85, and x is 80. What is the value of x?

Think of each value in terms of its position relative to the average, 80.

63 is 17 less than 80.

64 is 16 less than 80.

85 is 5 greater than 80.

So these three terms are a total of $17 + 16 - 5$, or 28, less than the average. Therefore, x must be 28 greater than the average to restore the balance at 80. So $x = 28 + 80 = 108$.

Average of Consecutive, Evenly Spaced Numbers

When consecutive numbers are evenly spaced, the average is the middle value. For example, the average of consecutive integers 6, 7, and 8 is 7.

If there is an even number of evenly spaced numbers, there is no single middle value. In that case, the average is midway between (that is, the average of) the middle two values. For example, the average of 5, 10, 15, and 20 is 12.5, midway between the middle values 10 and 15.

Note that not all consecutive numbers are evenly spaced. For instance, consecutive prime numbers arranged in increasing order are not evenly spaced. But you can use the handy technique of finding the middle value whenever you have consecutive integers, consecutive odd or even numbers, consecutive multiples of an integer, or any other consecutive numbers that are evenly spaced.

CHAPTER 3

Combining Averages

When there is an equal number of terms in each set, and *only when there is an equal number of terms in each set,* you can average averages.

For example, suppose there are two bowlers, and you must find their average score per game. One has an average score per game of 100, and the other has an average score per game of 200. If both bowlers bowled the same number of games, you can average their averages to find their combined average. Suppose they both bowled 4 games. Their combined average will be equally influenced by both bowlers. Hence, their combined average will be the average of 100 and 200. We can find this quickly by remembering that the quantity above the average and the quantity below the average must be equal. Therefore, the average will be halfway between 100 and 200, which is 150. Or, we could solve using our average formula:

$$\text{Average} = \frac{\text{Sum of terms}}{\text{Number of terms}} = \frac{4(100) + 4(200)}{8} = 150$$

However, if the bowler with the average score of 100 had bowled 4 games, and the bowler with the 200 average had bowled 16 games, the combined average would be weighted further toward 200 than toward 100, to reflect the greater influence of the 200 bowler than the 100 bowler upon the total. This is known as a *weighted average*.

Again, you can solve this by using the concept of a balanced average or by using the average formula.

Since the bowler bowling an average score of 200 bowled $\frac{4}{5}$ of the games, the combined average will be $\frac{4}{5}$ of the distance along the number line between 100 and 200, which is 180. Or, you can plug numbers into an average formula to find that

PROPORTIONS AND MATH FORMULAS

CHAPTER 3

$$\text{Average} = \frac{\text{Sum of terms}}{\text{Number of terms}}$$

$$\text{Average} = \frac{4(100) + 16(200)}{20}$$

$$\text{Average} = \frac{400 + 3200}{20}$$

$$\text{Average} = 180$$

Averages and Data Sufficiency

For Data Sufficiency average questions, you will have to scan the statements for any two elements of the average formula, from which you will know that you can find the third.

Example:

If the receipts for a matinee performance at the Granada Theater totaled $2,400, how many tickets were sold for that performance?

(1) The average price of a ticket sold was $7.50.

(2) All tickets sold cost either $10.00 or $6.00.

Use the average formula: $\text{Average} = \frac{\text{Sum of terms}}{\text{Number of terms}}$. In this case, you already know the sum of terms (total receipts = $2,400). All that you need to find the number of terms (number of tickets sold) is the other part of the equation: the average price of a ticket sold. Statement (1) gives you this information, so it is sufficient. Since you don't know how many $10.00 versus $6.00 tickets were sold, Statement (2) does not give you the number of tickets sold and so is not sufficient. The answer then is choice **(A)**.

CHAPTER 4

ALGEBRA

CHAPTER 4

Algebraic Terms

Variable: A letter or symbol representing an unknown quantity.

Constant (term): A number not multiplied by any variable(s).

Term: A numerical constant; also, the product of a numerical constant and one or more variables.

Coefficient: The numerical constant by which one or more variables are multiplied. The coefficient of $3x^2$ is 3. A variable (or product of variables) without a numerical coefficient, such as z or xy^3, is understood to have a coefficient of 1.

Algebraic expression: An expression containing one or more variables, one or more constants, and possibly one or more operation symbols. In the case of the expression x, there is an implied coefficient of 1. An expression does not contain an equals sign. x, $3x^2 + 2x$, and $\dfrac{7x + 1}{3x^2 - 14}$ are all algebraic expressions.

Monomial: An algebraic expression with only one term. To *multiply monomials*, multiply the coefficients and the variables separately: $2a \times 3a = (2 \times 3)(a \times a) = 6a^2$.

Polynomial: The general name for an algebraic expression with more than one term.

Algebraic equation: Two algebraic expressions separated by an equals sign, or one algebraic expression separated from a number by an equals sign.

CHAPTER 4

Basic Operations

Combining Like Terms

The process of simplifying an expression by adding together or subtracting terms that have the same variable factors is called *combining like terms*.

Example:

Simplify the expression $2x - 5y - x + 7y$.

$2x - 5y - x + 7y = (2x - x) + (7y - 5y) = x + 2y$

Notice that the commutative, associative, and distributive laws that govern arithmetic operations with ordinary numbers also apply to algebraic terms and polynomials.

Adding and Subtracting Polynomials

To *add or subtract polynomials*, combine like terms.

$(3x^2 + 5x + 7) - (x^2 + 12) = (3x^2 - x^2) + 5x + (7 - 12) = 2x^2 + 5x - 5$

CHAPTER 4

Factoring Algebraic Expressions

Factoring a polynomial means expressing it as a product of two or more simpler expressions. Common factors can be factored out by using the distributive law.

Example:

Factor the expression $2a + 6ac$.

The greatest common factor of $2a + 6ac$ is $2a$. Using the distributive law, you can factor out $2a$ so that the expression becomes $2a(1 + 3c)$.

Example:

All three terms in the polynomial $3x^3 + 12x^2 - 6x$ contain a factor of $3x$. Pulling out the common factor yields $3x(x^2 + 4x - 2)$.

CHAPTER 4

Advanced Operations

Substitution

Substitution, a process of plugging values into equations, is used to evaluate an algebraic expression or to express it in terms of other variables.

Replace every variable in the expression with the number or quantity you are told is its equivalent. Then carry out the designated operations, remembering to follow the order of operations (PEMDAS).

Example:

Express $\frac{a - b^2}{b - a}$ in terms of x if $a = 2x$ and $b = 3$.

Replace every a with $2x$ and every b with 3:

$$\frac{a - b^2}{b - a} = \frac{2x - 9}{3 - 2x}$$

Without more information, you can't simplify or evaluate this expression further.

Solving Equations

When you manipulate any equation, *always do the same thing on both sides of the equals sign*. Otherwise, the two sides of the equation will no longer be equal.

To solve an algebraic equation without exponents for a particular variable, you have to manipulate the equation until that variable is on one side of the equals sign, with all numbers or other variables on the other side. You can perform addition, subtraction, or multiplication; you can also perform division, as long as the quantity by which you are dividing does not equal zero.

ALGEBRA

CHAPTER 4

Typically, at each step of the process, you'll try to isolate the variable by using the reverse of whatever operation has been applied to the variable. For example, in solving the equation $n + 6 = 10$ for n, you have to get rid of the 6 that has been added to the n. You do that by subtracting 6 from both sides of the equation: $n + 6 - 6 = 10 - 6$, so $n = 4$.

Example:

If $4x - 7 = 2x + 5$, what is the value of x?

Start by adding 7 to both sides. This gives us $4x = 2x + 12$. Now subtract $2x$ from both sides. This gives us $2x = 12$. Finally, let's divide both sides by 2. This gives us $x = 6$.

Inequalities

There are two differences between solving an inequality (such as $2x < 5$) and solving an equation (such as $2x - 5 = 0$).

First, the solution to an inequality is almost always a range of possible values, rather than a single value. You can see the range easily by expressing it visually on a number line.

The shaded portion of the number line above shows the set of all numbers between -4 and 0 excluding the endpoints -4 and 0; this range would be expressed algebraically by the inequality $-4 < x < 0$.

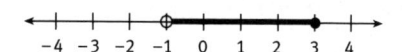

CHAPTER 4

The shaded portion of the number line above shows the set of all numbers greater than -1, up to and including 3; this range would be expressed algebraically by the inequality $-1 < x \leq 3$.

The other difference when solving an inequality—and the only thing you really have to remember—is that if you multiply or divide the inequality by a negative number, you have to reverse the direction of the inequality. For example, when you multiply both sides of the inequality $-3x < 2$ by -1, you get $3x > -2$.

Example:

Solve for x: $3 - \frac{x}{4} \geq 2$

Multiply both sides of the inequality by 4: $12 - x \geq 8$

Subtract 12 from both sides: $-x \geq -4$

Multiply (or divide) both sides by -1 and change the direction of the inequality sign: $x \leq 4$

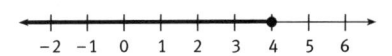

As you can see from the number line, the range of values that satisfies this inequality includes 4 and all numbers less than 4.

Solving for One Unknown in Terms of Another

In general, in order to solve for the value of an unknown, you need as many distinct equations as you have variables. If there are two variables, for instance, you need two distinct equations.

ALGEBRA

CHAPTER 4

However, some GMAT problems do not require you to solve for the numerical value of an unknown. Instead you are asked to solve for one variable in terms of the other(s). To do so, isolate the desired variable on one side of the equation and move all the constants and other variables to the other side.

Example:

In the formula $z = \dfrac{xy}{a + yb}$, solve for y in terms of x, z, a, and b.

Clear the denominator by multiplying both sides by $a + yb$:
$(a + yb)z = xy$

Remove parentheses by distributing: $az + ybz = xy$

Put all terms containing y on one side and all other terms on the other side: $az = xy - ybz$

Factor out the common factor, y: $az = y(x - bz)$

Divide by the coefficient of y to get y alone: $\dfrac{az}{x - bz} = y$

Simultaneous Equations

We've already discovered that you need as many different equations as you have variables to solve for the actual value of a variable. When a single equation contains more than one variable, you can only solve for one variable in terms of the others.

This has important implications for Data Sufficiency. For sufficiency, you usually must have at least as many equations as you have variables.

On the GMAT, you will often have to solve two simultaneous equations, that is, equations that give you different information about the same two variables. There are two methods for solving simultaneous equations.

Method 1—Substitution

Step 1: Solve one equation for one variable in terms of the second.

Step 2: Substitute the result back into the other equation and solve.

Example:

If $x - 15 = 2y$ and $6y + 2x = -10$, what is the value of y?

Solve the first equation for x by adding 15 to both sides.

$$x = 2y + 15$$

Substitute $2y + 15$ for x in the second equation:

$$6y + 2(2y + 15) = -10$$
$$6y + 4y + 30 = -10$$
$$10y = -40$$
$$y = -4$$

Method 2—Adding to Cancel

Combine the equations in such a way that one of the variables cancels out. To solve the two equations $4x + 3y = 8$ and $x + y = 3$, multiply both sides of the second equation by -3 to get $-3x - 3y = -9$. Now add the two equations; the $3y$ and the $-3y$ cancel out, leaving: $x = -1$.

Before you use either method, make sure you really do have two distinct equations. For example, $2x + 3y = 8$ and $4x + 6y = 16$ are really the same equation in different forms; multiply the first equation by 2, and you'll get the second.

Whichever method you use, you can check the result by plugging both values back into both equations and making sure they fit.

ALGEBRA

CHAPTER 4

Example:

If $m = 4n + 2$, and $3m + 2n = 16$, find the values of m and n.

Since the first equation already expresses m in terms of n, this problem is best approached by substitution.

Substitute $4n + 2$ for m into $3m + 2n = 16$, and solve for n.

$$3(4n + 2) + 2n = 16$$
$$12n + 6 + 2n = 16$$
$$14n = 10$$
$$n = \frac{5}{7}$$

Now solve either equation for m by plugging in for n.

$$m = 4n + 2$$
$$m = 4\left(\frac{5}{7}\right) + 2$$
$$m = \frac{20}{7} + 2$$
$$m = \frac{20}{7} + \frac{14}{7}$$
$$m = \frac{34}{7}$$

So $m = \frac{34}{7}$ and $n = \frac{5}{7}$.

Example:

If $3x + 3y = 18$ and $x - y = 10$, find the values of x and y.

You could solve this problem by the substitution method. But look what happens if you multiply the second equation by 3 and add it to the first:

$$3x + 3y = 18$$
$$+ (3x - 3y = 30)$$
$$6x = 48$$

If $6x = 48$, then $x = 8$. Now you can just plug 8 into either equation in place of x and solve for y. Your calculations will be simpler if you use the second equation: $8 - y = 10$; $-y = 2$; $y = -2$.

Simultaneous Equations in Data Sufficiency

Data Sufficiency questions will sometimes test your understanding of how many equations you need to solve for a variable.

Example:

What is the value of x?

(1) $x - 6y = 24$

(2) $4x + 2y = 16$

Neither statement alone is sufficient, since each equation allows you only to solve for x in terms of *another variable*. However, both statements together give two different equations with two unknowns—enough information to find the value of x. The answer is **(C)**.

Example:

What is the value of $x + y$?

(1) $x + 4y = -12$

(2) $5x + 5y = 18$

CHAPTER 4

We don't need the value of either variable by itself, but their sum. The second statement gives us enough information. If we divided both sides by 5, we could find the value of $x + y$. The answer is **(B)**.

Symbolism

Don't panic if you see strange symbols like *, ◇, and ♦ in a GMAT problem.

Problems of this type usually require nothing more than substitution. Read the question stem carefully for a definition of the symbols and for any examples of how to use them. Then, just follow the given model, substituting the numbers that are in the question stem.

Example:

An operation symbolized by ✻ is defined by the equation $x ✻ y = x - \frac{1}{y}$. What is the value of 2 ✻ 7?

The ✻ symbol is defined as a two-stage operation performed on two quantities, which are symbolized in the equation as x and y. The two steps are (1) find the reciprocal of the second quantity and (2) subtract the reciprocal from the first quantity. To find the value of 2 ✻ 7, substitute the numbers 2 and 7 into the equation, replacing the x (the first quantity given in the equation) with the 2 (the first number given) and the y (the second quantity given in the equation) with the 7 (the second number given). The reciprocal of 7 is $\frac{1}{7}$, and subtracting $\frac{1}{7}$ from 2 gives you

$$2 - \frac{1}{7} = \frac{14}{7} - \frac{1}{7} = \frac{13}{7}$$

CHAPTER 4

When a symbolism problem involves only one quantity, the operations are usually a little more complicated. Nonetheless, you can follow the same steps to find the correct answer.

Example:

Let $x*$ be defined by the equation: $x* = \dfrac{x^2}{1 - x^2}$. Evaluate $\left(\dfrac{1}{2}\right)*$.

$$\left(\dfrac{1}{2}\right)* = \dfrac{\left(\dfrac{1}{2}\right)^2}{1 - \left(\dfrac{1}{2}\right)^2} = \dfrac{\dfrac{1}{4}}{1 - \dfrac{1}{4}} = \dfrac{\dfrac{1}{4}}{\dfrac{3}{4}} = \dfrac{1}{4} \times \dfrac{4}{3} = \dfrac{1}{3}$$

Every once in a while, you'll see a symbolism problem that doesn't even include an equation. The definitions in this type of problem usually test your understanding of number properties.

Example:

✲x is defined as the largest even number that is less than the negative square root of x. What is the value of ✲81?

- ○ −82
- ○ −80
- ○ −10
- ○ −8
- ○ 8

Plug in 81 for x and work backward logically. The negative square root of 81 is −9 because (−9)(−9) = 81. The largest even number that is less than −9 is −10. (The number part of −8 is smaller than the number part of −9; however, you're dealing with negative numbers, so you have to look for the even number that would be just to the *left* of −9 along the number line.) Thus, the correct answer choice is **(C)**, −10.

ALGEBRA KAPLAN 83

CHAPTER 4

Sequences

Sequences are lists of numbers. The value of a number in a sequence is related to its position in the list. Sequences are often represented on the GMAT as follows:

$$s_1, s_2, s_3, \ldots s_n, \ldots$$

The subscript part of each number gives you the position of each element in the series. s_1 is the first number in the list. s_2 is the second number in the list, and so on.

You will be given a formula that defines each element. For example, if you are told that $s_n = 2n + 1$, then the sequence would be $(2 \times 1) + 1, (2 \times 2) + 1, (2 \times 3) + 1, \ldots$, or $3, 5, 7, \ldots$

CHAPTER 4

Polynomials and Quadratics

The FOIL Method

When two binomials are multiplied, each term is multiplied by each term in the other binomial. This process is often called the FOIL method, because it involves adding the products of the First, Outer, Inner, and Last terms. Using the FOIL method to multiply out $(x + 5)(x - 2)$, the product of the first terms is x^2, the product of the outer terms is $-2x$, the product of the inner terms is $5x$, and the product of the last terms is -10. Adding, the answer is $x^2 + 3x - 10$.

Factoring the Product of Binomials

Many of the polynomials that you'll see on the GMAT can be factored into a product of two binomials by using the FOIL method backwards.

Example:

Factor the polynomial $x^2 - 3x + 2$.

You can factor this into two binomials, each containing an x term. Start by writing down what you know:

$$x^2 - 3x + 2 = (x\quad)(x\quad)$$

You'll need to fill in the missing term in each binomial factor. The product of the two missing terms will be the last term in the original polynomial: 2. The sum of the two missing terms will be the coefficient of the second term of the polynomial: -3. Find the factors of 2 that add up to -3. Since $(-1) + (-2) = -3$, you can fill the empty spaces with -1 and -2.

Thus, $x^2 - 3x + 2 = (x - 1)(x - 2)$.

ALGEBRA

CHAPTER 4

Note: Whenever you factor a polynomial, you can check your answer by using FOIL to multiply the factors and obtain the original polynomial.

Factoring the Difference of Two Squares

A common factorable expression on the GMAT is the difference of two squares (for example, $a^2 - b^2$). Once you recognize a polynomial as the difference of two squares, you'll be able to factor it automatically, since any polynomial of the form $a^2 - b^2$ can be factored into a product of the form $(a + b)(a - b)$.

Example:

Factor the expression $9x^2 - 1$.

$9x^2 = (3x)^2$ and $1 = 1^2$, so $9x^2 - 1$ is the difference of two squares.

Therefore, $9x^2 - 1 = (3x + 1)(3x - 1)$.

Factoring Polynomials of the Form $a^2 + 2ab + b^2$

Any polynomial of this form is the square of a binomial expression, as you can see by using the FOIL method to multiply $(a + b)(a + b)$ or $(a - b)(a - b)$.

To factor a polynomial of this form, check the sign in front of the $2ab$ term. If it's a *plus* sign, the polynomial is equal to $(a + b)^2$. If it's a *minus* sign, the polynomial is equal to $(a - b)^2$.

Example:

Factor the polynomial $x^2 + 6x + 9$.

x^2 and 9 are both perfect squares, and $6x$ is $2(3x)$, which is twice the product of x and 3, so this polynomial is of the form $a^2 + 2ab + b^2$ with $a = x$ and $b = 3$. Since there is a plus sign in front of the $6x$, $x^2 + 6x + 9 = (x + 3)^2$.

CHAPTER 4

Quadratic Equations

A quadratic equation is an equation of the form $ax^2 + bx + c = 0$. Many quadratic equations have two solutions. In other words, the equation will be true for two different values of x.

When you see a quadratic equation on the GMAT, you'll generally be able to solve it by factoring the algebraic expression, setting each of the factors equal to zero, and solving the resulting equations.

Example:

$x^2 - 3x + 2 = 0$. Solve for x.

To find the solutions, or roots, start by factoring $x^2 - 3x + 2 = 0$ into $(x - 2)(x - 1) = 0$.

The product of two quantities equals zero only if one (or both) of the quantities equals zero. So if you set each of the factors equal to zero, you will be able to solve the resulting equations for the solutions of the original quadratic equation. Setting the two binomials equal to zero gives you

$$x - 2 = 0 \quad \text{or} \quad x - 1 = 0$$

That means that x can equal 2 or 1. As a check, you can plug each of those values in turn into $x^2 - 3x + 2 = 0$, and you'll see that either value makes the equation work.

ALGEBRA

CHAPTER 4

Alternative Strategies for Multiple-Choice Algebra

Backsolving

On GMAT Problem Solving questions, you may find it easier to attack algebra problems by Backsolving.

To backsolve, substitute each answer choice into the equation until you find the one that satisfies the equation.

Example:

If $x^2 + 10x + 25 = 0$, what is the value of x?

- ○ 25
- ○ 10
- ○ 5
- ○ −5
- ○ −10

The textbook approach to solve this problem would be to recognize the polynomial expression as the square of the binomial $(x + 5)$ and set $x + 5 = 0$. That's the fastest way to arrive at the correct answer of −5.

But you could also plug each answer choice into the equation until you found the one that makes the equation true. Backsolving can be pretty quick if the correct answer is the first choice you plug in, but here, you have to get all the way down to choice **(D)** before you find that $(-5)^2 + 10(-5) + 25 = 0$.

CHAPTER 4

Example:

If $\frac{5x}{3} + 9 = \frac{x}{6} + 18$, $x =$

○ 12
○ 8
○ 6
○ 5
○ 4

To avoid having to try all five answer choices, look at the equation and decide which choice(s), if plugged in for x, would make your calculations easiest. Since x is in the numerators of the two fractions in this equation, and the denominators are 3 and 6, try plugging in a choice that is divisible by both 3 and 6. Choices **(A)** and **(C)** are divisible by both numbers, so start with one of them.

Choice **(A)**:

$$20 + 9 = 2 + 18$$
$$29 \neq 20$$

This is not true, so x cannot equal 12.

Choice **(C)**:

$$10 + 9 = 1 + 18$$
$$19 = 19$$

This is correct, so x must equal 6. Therefore, choice **(C)** is correct.

Backsolving may not be the fastest method for a multiple-choice algebra problem, but it's useful if you don't think you'll be able to solve the problem in the conventional way.

CHAPTER

4

Picking Numbers

On other types of multiple-choice algebra problems, especially where the answer choices consist of variables or algebraic expressions, you may want to pick numbers to make the problem less abstract. Evaluate the answer choices and the information in the question stem by picking a number and substituting it for the variable wherever the variable appears.

Example:

If $a > 1$, the ratio of $2a + 6$ to $a^2 + 2a - 3$ is

- ○ $2a$
- ○ $a + 3$
- ○ $\dfrac{2}{a - 1}$
- ○ $\dfrac{2a}{3(3 - a)}$
- ○ $\dfrac{a - 1}{2}$

You can simplify the process by replacing the variable a with a number in each algebraic expression. Since a has to be greater than 1, why not pick 2? Then the expression $2a + 6$ becomes $2(2) + 6$, or 10. The expression $a^2 + 2a - 3$ becomes $2^2 + 2(2) - 3 = 4 + 4 - 3 = 5$.

So now the question reads, "the ratio of 10 to 5 is what?" That's easy enough to answer: 10:5 is the same as $\dfrac{10}{5}$, or 2. Now you can just eliminate any answer choice that doesn't give a result of 2 when you substitute 2 for a. Choice **(A)** gives you 2(2), or 4, so discard it. Choice **(B)** results in 5—also not what you want. Choice **(C)** yields $\dfrac{2}{1}$ or 2. That looks good, but you can't stop here.

MATH

90   KAPLAN   ALGEBRA

CHAPTER 4

If another answer choice gives you a result of 2, you will have to pick another number for a and reevaluate the expressions in the question stem and the choices that worked when you let $a = 2$.

Choice **(D)** gives you $\frac{2(2)}{3(3-2)}$ or $\frac{4}{3}$, so eliminate choice **(D)**.

Choice **(E)** gives you $\frac{2-1}{2}$ or $\frac{1}{2}$, so discard choice **(E)**.

Fortunately, in this case, only choice **(C)** works out equal to 2, so it is the correct answer. But remember: When Picking Numbers, always check every answer choice to make sure you haven't chosen a number that works for more than one answer choice.

Using Picking Numbers to Solve for One Unknown in Terms of Another

It is also possible to solve for one unknown in terms of another by Picking Numbers. If the first number you pick doesn't lead to a single correct answer, be prepared to either pick a new number (and spend more time on the problem) or settle for guessing strategically among the answers that you haven't eliminated.

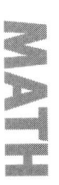

ALGEBRA

CHAPTER 4

Example:

If $\dfrac{x^2 - 16}{x^2 + 6x + 8} = y$ and $x > -2$, which of the following is an expression for x in terms of y?

○ $\dfrac{1 + y}{2 - y}$

○ $\dfrac{2y + 4}{1 - y}$

○ $\dfrac{4y - 4}{y + 1}$

○ $\dfrac{2y - 4}{2 + y}$

○ $\dfrac{y + 4}{y + 1}$

Pick a value for x that will simplify your calculations. If you let x equal 4, then $x^2 - 16 = 4^2 - 16 = 0$, and so the entire fraction on the left side of the equation is equal to zero.

Now, substitute 0 for y in each answer choice in turn. Each choice is an expression for x in terms of y, and since $y = 0$ when $x = 4$, the correct answer will have to give a value of 4 when $y = 0$. Just remember to evaluate all the answer choices, because you might find more than one that gives a result of 4.

Substituting 0 for y in choices **(A)**, **(C)**, and **(D)** yields $\dfrac{1}{2}$, $-\dfrac{4}{1}$, and $-\dfrac{4}{2}$, respectively, so none of those choices can be right.

But both **(B)** and **(E)** give results of 4 when you make the substitution; choosing between them will require picking another number.

CHAPTER 4

Again, pick a number that will make calculations easy. If $x = 0$, then $y =$

$$\frac{x^2 - 16}{x^2 + 6x + 8} = \frac{0 - 16}{0 + 0 + 8} = \frac{-16}{8} = -2$$

Therefore, $y = -2$ when $x = 0$. You don't have to try the new value of y in all the answer choices, just in **(B)** and **(E)**. When you substitute -2 for y in choice **(B)**, you get 0. That's what you're looking for, but again, you have to make sure it doesn't work in choice **(E)**. Plugging -2 in for y in **(E)** yields -2 for x, so **(B)** was correct.

ALGEBRA

CHAPTER 5

STATISTICS

CHAPTER 5

Median, Mode, and Range

Median: The middle term in a group of terms that are arranged in numerical order. To find the median of a group of terms, first arrange the terms in numerical order. If there is an odd number of terms in the group, then the median is the middle term.

Example:

Bob's test scores in Spanish are 84, 81, 88, 70, and 87. What is his median score?

In increasing order, his scores are 70, 81, 84, 87, and 88. The median test score is the middle one: 84.

If there is an even number of terms in the group, the median is the average of the two middle terms.

Example:

John's test scores in biology are 92, 98, 82, 94, 85, 97. What is his median score?

In numerical order, his scores are 82, 85, 92, 94, 97, and 98. The median test score is the average of the two middle terms, or $\frac{92 + 94}{2} = 93$.

CHAPTER 5

The median of a group of numbers is often different from its average.

Example:

Caitlin's test scores in math are 92, 96, 90, 85, and 82. Find the difference between Caitlin's median score and the average (arithmetic mean) of her scores.

In ascending order, Caitlin's scores are 82, 85, 90, 92, and 96. The median score is the middle one: 90. Her average score is $\frac{82 + 85 + 90 + 92 + 96}{5} = \frac{445}{5} = 89$.

As you can see, Caitlin's median score and average score are not the same. The difference between them is $90 - 89$, or 1.

Mode: The term that appears most frequently in a set.

Example:

The daily temperatures in city Q for one week were 25°, 33°, 26°, 25°, 27°, 31°, and 22°. What was the mode of the daily temperatures in city Q for that week?

Each of the temperatures occurs once on the list, except for 25°, which occurs twice. Since 25° appears more frequently than any other temperature, it is the mode.

STATISTICS

CHAPTER 5

A set may have more than one mode if two or more terms appear an equal number of times within the set and each appears more times than any other term.

Example:

The table below represents the score distribution for a class of 20 students on a recent chemistry test. Which score, or scores, are the mode?

Score	# of Students Receiving That Score
100	2
91	1
87	5
86	2
85	1
84	5
80	1
78	2
56	1

The largest number in the second column is 5, which occurs twice. Therefore, there were two mode scores on this test: 87 and 84. Equal numbers of students received those scores, and more students received those scores than any other score.

If every element in the set occurs an equal number of times, then the set has no mode.

CHAPTER

5

Combination

A combination question asks you how many unordered subgroups can be formed from a larger group.

Some combination questions on the GMAT can be solved without any computation just by counting or listing possible combinations.

Example:

Allen, Betty, and Claire must wash the dishes. They decide to work in shifts of two people. How many shifts will it take before all possible combinations have been used?

It is possible, and not time-consuming, to solve this problem by writing a list. Call Allen "*A*," Betty "*B*," and Claire "*C*." There are three (*AB, AC, BC*) possible combinations.

The Combination Formula

Some combination questions use numbers that make quick, noncomputational solving difficult. In these cases, use the combination formula $\frac{n!}{k!(n-k)!}$, where *n* is the number of items in the group as a whole and *k* is the number of items in each subgroup formed. The ! symbol means factorial (for example, $5! = (5)(4)(3)(2)(1) = 120$).

Example:

The 4 finalists in a spelling contest win commemorative plaques. If there are 7 entrants in the spelling contest, how many possible groups of winners are there?

Plug the numbers into the combination formula, such that n is 7 (the number in the large group) and k is 4 (the number of people in each subgroup formed).

$$\frac{7!}{4!(7-4)!}$$

$$\frac{7!}{4!3!}$$

At this stage, it is helpful to reduce these terms. Since 7 factorial contains all the factors of 4 factorial, we can write 7! as (7)(6)(5)(4!) and then cancel the 4! in the numerator and denominator.

$$\frac{(7)(6)(5)}{(3)(2)(1)} = ?$$

We can reduce further by crossing off the 6 in the numerator and the (3)(2) in the denominator.

$$\frac{(7)(5)}{1} = 35$$

There are 35 potential groups of spelling contest finalists.

When you are asked to find potential combinations from multiple groups, multiply the potential combinations from each group.

Example:

How many groups can be formed consisting of 2 people from room A and 3 people from room B if there are 5 people in room A and 6 people in room B?

Insert the appropriate numbers into the combination formula for each room and then multiply the results. For room A, the number of combinations of 2 in a set of 5 is

CHAPTER 5

$\dfrac{n!}{k!(n-k)!} = \dfrac{5!}{2!3!} = \dfrac{(5)(4)(3)(2)(1)}{(2)(1)(3)(2)(1)}$. Reducing this you get $\dfrac{(5)(4)}{(2)} = 10$. For room B, the number of combinations of 3 in a set of 6 is $\dfrac{n!}{k!(n-k)!} = \dfrac{6!}{3!3!} = \dfrac{(6)(5)(4)(3)(2)(1)}{(3)(2)(1)(3)(2)(1)}$. Reducing this you get $\dfrac{(6)(5)(4)}{(3)(2)} = 20$.

Multiply these to find that there are $(10)(20) = 200$ possible groups consisting of 2 people from room A and 3 people from room B.

Sometimes the GMAT will ask you to find the number of possible subgroups when choosing one item from a set. In this case, the number of possible subgroups will always equal the number of items in the set.

Example:

Restaurant A has 5 appetizers, 20 main courses, and 4 desserts. If a meal consists of 1 appetizer, 1 main course, and 1 dessert, how many different meals can be ordered at restaurant A?

The number of possible outcomes from each set is the number of items in the set. So there are 5 possible appetizers, 20 possible main courses, and 4 possible desserts. The number of different meals that can be ordered is $(5)(20)(4) = 400$.

CHAPTER

5

Permutation

Within any group of items or people, there are multiple arrangements, or permutations, possible. For instance, within a group of three items (for example: *A, B, C*), there are six permutations (*ABC, ACB, BAC, BCA, CAB,* and *CBA*).

Permutations differ from combinations in that permutations are ordered. By definition, each combination larger than 1 has multiple permutations. On the GMAT, a question asking "How many ways/arrangements/orders/schedules are possible?" generally indicates a permutation problem.

To find permutations, think of each place that needs to be filled in a particular arrangement as a blank space. The first place can be filled with any of the items in the larger group. The second place can be filled with any of the items in the larger group except for the one used to fill the first place. The third place can be filled with any of the items in the group except for the two used to fill the first two places, etc.

Example:

In a spelling contest, the winner will receive a gold medal, the second-place finisher will receive a silver medal, the third-place finisher will receive a bronze medal, and the fourth-place finisher will receive a blue ribbon. If there are 7 entrants in the contest, how many different arrangements of award winners are there?

The gold medal can be won by any of 7 people. The silver medal can be won by any of the remaining (6) people. The bronze medal can be won by any of the remaining (5) people. And the blue ribbon can be won by any of the remaining (4) people. Thus, the number of possible arrangements is (7)(6)(5)(4) = 840.

CHAPTER 5

Probability

Probability is the numerical representation of the likelihood of an event or combination of events. This is expressed as a ratio of the number of desired outcomes to the total number of possible outcomes. Probability is usually expressed as a fraction (for example "the probability of event A occurring is $\frac{1}{3}$), but it can also be expressed in words ("the probability of event A occurring is 1 in 3"). The probability of any event occurring cannot exceed 1 (a probability of 1 represents a 100% chance of an event occurring), and it cannot be less than 0 (a probability of 0 represents a 0% chance of an event occurring).

Example:

If you flip a fair coin, what is the probability that it will fall with the "heads" side facing up?

The probability of the coin landing heads up is $\frac{1}{2}$, since there is one outcome you are interested in (landing heads up) and two possible outcomes (heads up or tails up).

Example:

What is the probability of rolling a 5 or a 6 on a six-sided die numbered 1 through 6 ?

The probability of rolling a 5 or a 6 on a six-sided die numbered 1 through 6 is $\frac{2}{6} = \frac{1}{3}$, since there are 2 desired outcomes (rolling a 5 or a 6) and 6 possible outcomes (rolling a 1, 2, 3, 4, 5, or 6).

CHAPTER 5

The sum of all possible outcomes, desired or otherwise, must equal 1. In other words, if there is a 25% chance that event *A* will occur, then there is a 75% chance that it will not occur. So, to find the probability that an event *does not* occur, subtract the probability that it *does* occur from 1. In the previous example, the probability of not throwing a 5 or a 6 on the die is

$1 - \frac{1}{3} = \frac{2}{3}$.

When events are independent, that is, the events do not depend on the other event or events, the probability that several events all occur is the product of the probability of each event occurring individually.

Example:

A fair coin is flipped twice. What is the probability of its landing with the heads side facing up on both flips?

Multiply the probability for each flip: $\left(\frac{1}{2}\right)\left(\frac{1}{2}\right) = \frac{1}{4}$.

CHAPTER 5

Probability of Dependent Events

In some situations, the probability of a later event occurring varies according to the results of an earlier event. In this case, the probability fraction for the later event must be adjusted accordingly.

Example:

A bag contains 10 marbles, 4 of which are blue, and 6 of which are red. If 2 marbles are removed without replacement, what is the probability that both marbles removed are red?

The probability that the first marble removed will be red is $\frac{6}{10} = \frac{3}{5}$.

The probability that the second marble removed will be red will not be the same, however. There will be fewer marbles overall, so the denominator will be one less. There will also be one fewer red marble. (Note that since we are asking about the odds of picking two red marbles, we are only interested in choosing a second marble if the first was red. Don't concern yourself with situations in which a blue marble is chosen first.) If the first marble removed is red, the probability that the second marble removed will also be red is $\frac{5}{9}$. So the probability that both marbles removed will be red is $\left(\frac{3}{5}\right)\left(\frac{5}{9}\right) = \frac{15}{45} = \frac{1}{3}$.

CHAPTER 6

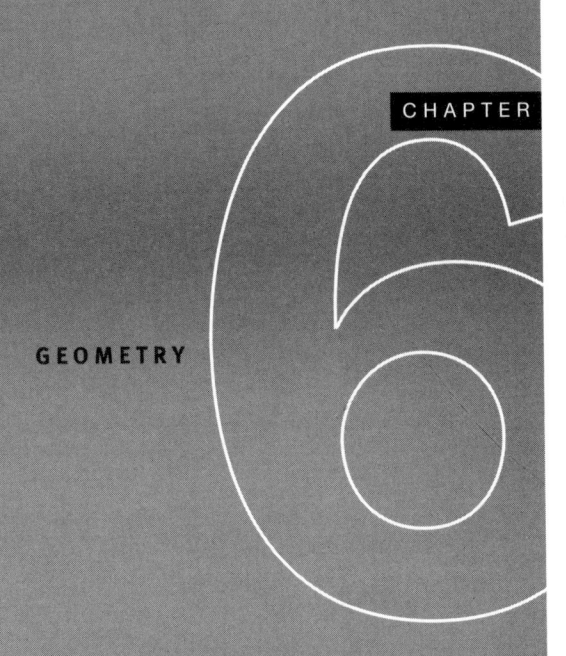

GEOMETRY

CHAPTER

6

Lines and Angles

A **line** is a one-dimensional geometrical abstraction—infinitely long, with no width. A straight line is the shortest distance between any two points. There is exactly one straight line that passes through any two points.

```
  A     B        C           D
  •─────•────────•───────────•
```

Example:

In the figure above, $AC = 9$, $BD = 11$, and $AD = 15$. What is the length of BC?

When points are in a line and the order is known, you can add or subtract lengths. Since $AC = 9$ and $AD = 15$, $CD = AD - AC = 15 - 9 = 6$. Now, since $BD = 11$ and $CD = 6$, $BC = BD - CD = 11 - 6 = 5$.

A **line segment** is a section of a straight line, of finite length, with two endpoints. A line segment is named for its endpoints, as in segment AB.

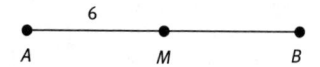

```
        6
  •─────────•─────────────•
  A         M             B
```

Example:

In the figure above, A and B are the endpoints of the line segment AB, and M is the midpoint ($AM = MB$). What is the length of AB?

Since AM is 6, MB is also 6, and so AB is $6 + 6$, or 12.

Two lines are **parallel** if they lie in the same plane and never intersect regardless of how far they are extended. If line ℓ_1 is parallel to line ℓ_2,

108 **KAPLAN**

GEOMETRY

CHAPTER 6

we write $\ell_1 \parallel \ell_2$. If two lines are both parallel to a third line, then they are parallel to each other as well.

A **vertex** is the point at which two lines or line segments intersect to form an **angle**. Angles are measured in **degrees** (°).

Angles may be named according to their vertices. Sometimes, especially when two or more angles share a common vertex, an angle is named according to three points: a point along one of the lines or line segments that form the angle, the vertex point, and another point along the other line or line segment. A diagram will sometimes show a letter inside the angle; this letter may also be used to name the angle.

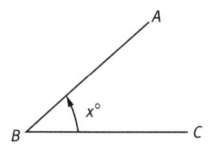

The angle shown in the diagram above could be called $\angle x$, $\angle ABC$, or $\angle B$. (We use a lowercase x because x is not a point.)

Sum of Angles Around a Point

The sum of the measures of the angles around a point is 360°.

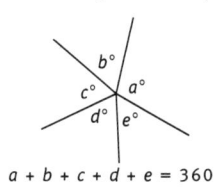

$$a + b + c + d + e = 360$$

GEOMETRY

CHAPTER 6

Sum of Angles Along a Straight Line

The sum of the measures of the angles on one side of a straight line is 180°. Two angles are *supplementary* to each other if their measures sum to 180°.

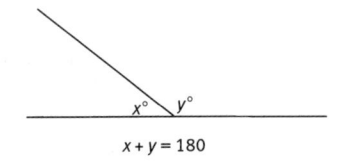

$x + y = 180$

Perpendicularity and Right Angles

Two lines are perpendicular if they intersect at a 90° angle (a right angle). If line ℓ_1 is perpendicular to line ℓ_2, we write $\ell_1 \perp \ell_2$. If lines ℓ_1, ℓ_2, and ℓ_3 all lie in the same plane, and $\ell_1 \perp \ell_2$ and $\ell_2 \perp \ell_3$, then $\ell_1 \parallel \ell_3$, as shown in the diagram below.

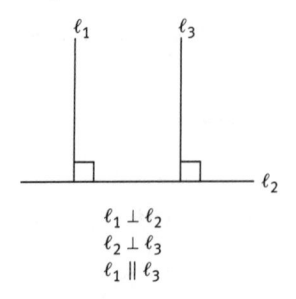

$\ell_1 \perp \ell_2$
$\ell_2 \perp \ell_3$
$\ell_1 \parallel \ell_3$

To find the shortest distance from a point to a line, draw a line segment from the point to the line such that the line segment is perpendicular to the line. Then, measure the length of that segment.

CHAPTER 6

Example:

∠A of triangle ABC is a right angle. Is side BC longer or shorter than side AB?

This question seems very abstract, until you draw a diagram of a right triangle, labeling the vertex with the 90° angle as point A.

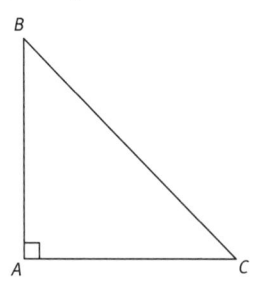

Line segment AB has to be the shortest route between point B and side AC, since side AB is perpendicular to side AC. If AB is the shortest line segment that can join point B to side AC, BC must be longer than AB. **Note:** The side opposite the 90° angle, called the *hypotenuse*, is always the longest side of a right triangle.

Two angles are *complementary* to each other if their measures sum to 90°. An *acute angle* measures less than 90°, and an *obtuse angle* measures between 90° and 180°. Two angles are *supplementary* if their measures sum to 180°.

CHAPTER 6

Angle Bisectors

A line or line segment bisects an angle if it splits the angle into two smaller, equal angles. Line segment BD below bisects $\angle ABC$, and $\angle ABD$ has the same measure as $\angle DBC$. The two smaller angles are each half the size of $\angle ABC$.

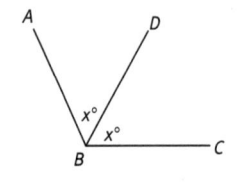

BD bisects $\angle ABC$

$\angle ABD + \angle DBC = \angle ABC$

Adjacent and Vertical Angles

Two intersecting lines form four angles. The angles that are adjacent (next) to each other are *supplementary* because they lie along a straight line. The two angles that are not adjacent to each other are *opposite*, or *vertical*. Opposite angles are equal in measure because each of them is supplementary to the same adjacent angle.

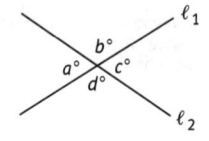

In the diagram above, ℓ_1 intersects ℓ_2 to form angles a, b, c, and d. Angles a and c are opposite, as are angles b and d. So the measures of angles *a* and *c* are equal to each other, and the measures of angles *b* and *d* are equal to each other. And each angle is supplementary to each of its two adjacent angles.

Angles Around Parallel Lines Intersected by a Transversal

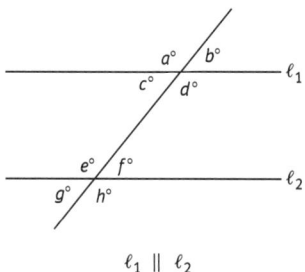

$\ell_1 \parallel \ell_2$

A line that intersects two parallel lines is called a *transversal*. Each of the parallel lines intersects the third line at the same angle. In the figure above, $a = e$. Since a and e are equal, and since $a = d$ and $e = h$ (because they are opposite angles), $a = d = e = h$. By similar reasoning, $b = c = f = g$.

In short, when two (or more) parallel lines are cut by a transversal: all acute angles formed are equal; all obtuse angles formed are equal; and any acute angle formed is supplementary to any obtuse angle formed.

CHAPTER 6

Example:

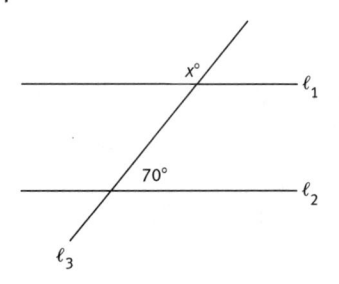

In the diagram above, line ℓ_1 is parallel to line ℓ_2. What is the value of x?

The angle marked $x°$ and the angle adjacent and to the left of the 70° angle on line ℓ_2 are corresponding angles. Therefore, the angle marked $x°$ must be supplementary to the 70° angle. If $70° + x° = 180°$, x must equal 110.

CHAPTER 6

Polygons

Important Terms

Polygon: A closed figure whose sides are straight line segments. Families or classes of polygons are named according to the number of sides. A triangle has three sides; a quadrilateral has four sides; a pentagon has five sides; and a hexagon has six sides. Triangles and quadrilaterals are by far the most important polygons on the GMAT; other polygons appear only occasionally.

Perimeter: The distance around a polygon; the sum of the lengths of its sides.

Vertex of a polygon: A point where two sides intersect; *pl.* vertices. Polygons are named by assigning each vertex a letter and listing them in order, as in pentagon *ABCDE* below.

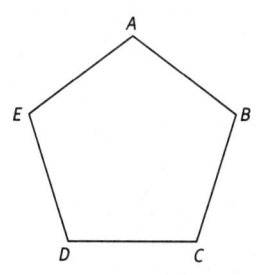

Diagonal of a polygon: A line segment connecting any two nonadjacent vertices.

Regular polygon: A polygon with sides of equal length and interior angles of equal measure.

CHAPTER 6

Small slash marks can provide important information in diagrams of polygons. Sides with the same number of slash marks are equal in length, while angles with the same number of slash marks through circular arcs have the same measure. In the triangle below, for example, $a = b$, and angles X and Z are equal in measure.

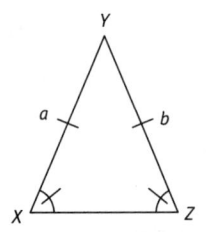

You can figure out the sum of the interior angles of a polygon by dividing the polygon into triangles. Draw diagonals from any vertex to all the nonadjacent vertices. Then, multiply the number of triangles by 180° to get the sum of the interior angles of the polygon. This works because the sum of the interior angles of any triangle is always 180°.

CHAPTER 6

Example:

What is the sum of the interior angles of a pentagon?

Draw a pentagon (a five-sided polygon) and divide it into triangles, as discussed above.

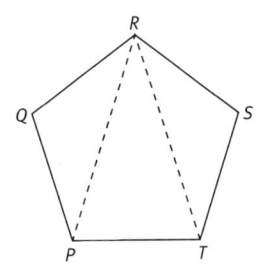

No matter how you've drawn the pentagon, you'll be able to form three triangles. Therefore, the sum of the interior angles of a pentagon is $3 \times 180° = 540°$.

CHAPTER 6

Triangles

Important Terms

Triangle: A polygon with three straight sides and three interior angles.

Right triangle: A triangle with one interior angle of 90° (a right angle).

Hypotenuse: The longest side of a right triangle. The hypotenuse is always opposite the right angle.

Isosceles triangle: A triangle with two equal sides, which are opposite two equal angles. In the figure below, the sides opposite the two 70° angles are equal, so $x = 7$.

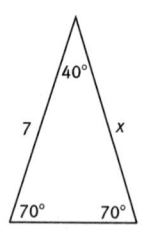

Legs: The two equal sides of an isosceles triangle, or the two shorter sides of a right triangle (the ones forming the right angle). **Note:** The third, unequal side of an isosceles triangle is called the *base*.

CHAPTER 6

Equilateral triangle: A triangle whose three sides are all equal in length and whose three interior angles each measure 60°.

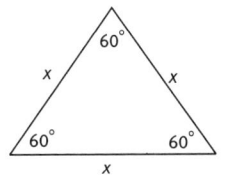

The **altitude,** or **height,** of a triangle is the perpendicular distance from a vertex to the side opposite the vertex. The altitude may fall inside or outside the triangle, or it may coincide with one of the sides.

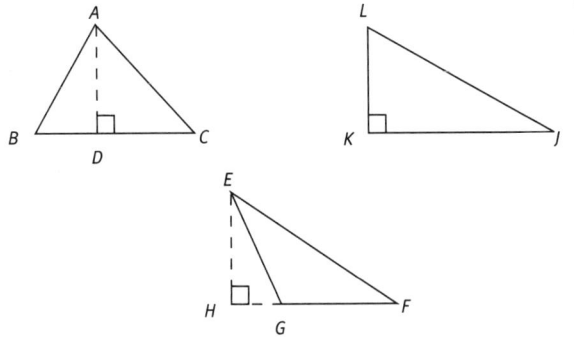

In the diagrams above, *AD*, *EH*, and *LK* are altitudes.

CHAPTER 6

Interior and Exterior Angles of a Triangle

The sum of the interior angles of any triangle is 180°. Therefore, in the figure below, $a + b + c = 180$.

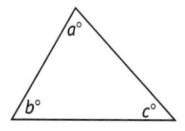

An *exterior angle of a triangle* is equal to the sum of the remote interior angles. The exterior angle labeled $x°$ is equal to the sum of the remote angles: $x = 50 + 100 = 150$.

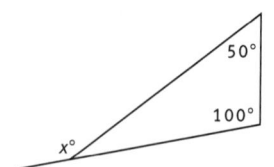

The three exterior angles of any triangle add up to 360°.

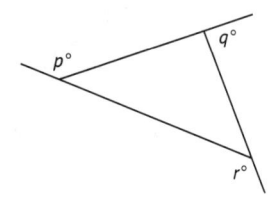

In the figure above, $p + q + r = 360$.

CHAPTER 6

Sides and Angles

The sum of the lengths of any two sides of a triangle is greater than the length of the third side. In the triangle below, $b + c > a$, $a + b > c$, and $a + c > b$.

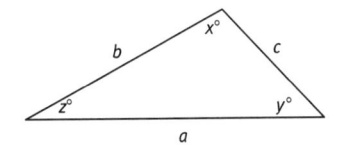

If the lengths of two sides of a triangle are unequal, the greater angle lies opposite the longer side, and vice versa. In the figure above, if $x > y > z$, then $a > b > c$.

Since the two legs of an isosceles triangle have the same length, the two angles opposite the legs must have the same measure. In the figure below, $PQ = PR$, and $\angle Q = \angle R$.

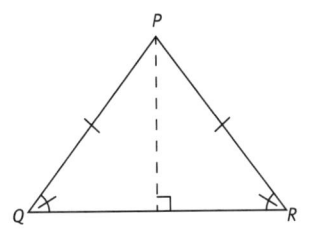

GEOMETRY

CHAPTER

6

Perimeter and Area of Triangles

There is no special formula for the perimeter of a triangle; it is just the sum of the lengths of the sides.

Example:

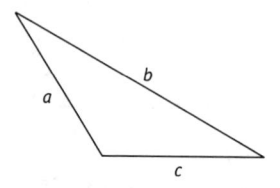

If $b = 2a$ and $c = \frac{b}{2}$, find the perimeter of the triangle above in terms of a.

Perimeter $= a + b + c = a + 2a + \frac{2a}{2} = 3a + \frac{2a}{2} = 3a + a = 4a$.

Incidentally, this is really an isosceles triangle, since $c = \frac{b}{2} = \frac{2a}{2} = a$.

CHAPTER 6

The area of a triangle is $\left(\frac{1}{2}\right)$(Base)(Height).

Example:

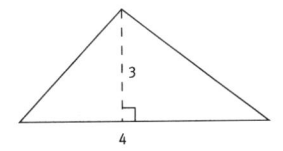

In the diagram above, the base has length 4 and the altitude has length 3. What is the area of the triangle?

$$\text{Area} = \frac{1}{2} bh$$
$$= \frac{bh}{2}$$
$$= \frac{4 \times 3}{2}$$
$$= 6$$

Since the lengths of the base and altitude were not given in specific units, such as centimeters or feet, the area of the triangle is simply said to be 6 square units.

The area of a right triangle is easy to find. Think of one leg as the base and the other as the height. Then the area is one-half the product of the legs, or $\frac{1}{2} \times \text{Leg}_1 \times \text{Leg}_2$.

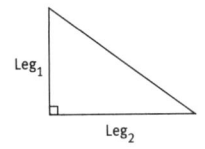

GEOMETRY

CHAPTER 6

Right Triangles

The right angle is always the largest angle in a right triangle; therefore, the hypotenuse, which lies opposite the right angle, is always the longest side.

Pythagorean Theorem

The Pythagorean theorem, which holds for all right triangles and for no other triangles, states that the square of the hypotenuse is equal to the sum of the squares of the legs.

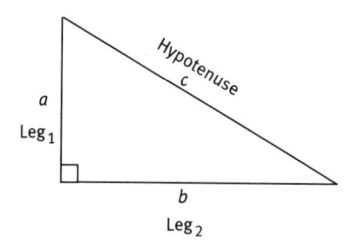

$(Leg_1)^2 + (Leg_2)^2 = (Hypotenuse)^2$

or $a^2 + b^2 = c^2$

The Pythagorean theorem is very useful whenever you're given the lengths of any two sides of a right triangle; as long as you know whether the remaining side is a leg or the hypotenuse, you can find its length by using the Pythagorean theorem.

CHAPTER 6

Example:

What is the length of the hypotenuse of a right triangle with legs of lengths 9 and 10?

$$(\text{Hypotenuse})^2 = (\text{Leg}_1)^2 + (\text{Leg}_2)^2$$
$$= 9^2 + 10^2$$
$$= 81 + 100$$
$$= 181$$

If the square of the hypotenuse equals 181, then the hypotenuse itself must be the square root of 181, or $\sqrt{181}$.

Pythagorean Triples

Certain ratios of integers always satisfy the Pythagorean theorem. You might like to think of them as "Pythagorean triples." One such ratio is 3, 4, and 5. A right triangle with legs of lengths 3 and 4 and hypotenuse of length 5 is probably the most common kind of right triangle on the GMAT. Whenever you see a right triangle with legs of 3 and 4, with a leg of 3 and a hypotenuse of 5, or with a leg of 4 and a hypotenuse of 5, you immediately know the length of the remaining side. In addition, any multiple of these lengths makes another Pythagorean triple; for instance, $6^2 + 8^2 = 10^2$, so a triangle with sides of lengths 6, 8, and 10 is also a right triangle.

The other triple that commonly appears on the GMAT is 5, 12, and 13.

CHAPTER

6

Special Right Triangles

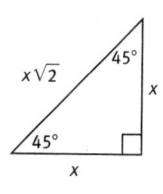

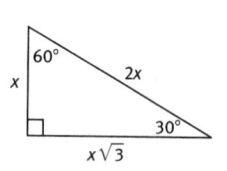

There are two more special kinds of right triangles for which you won't have to use the Pythagorean theorem to find the lengths of the sides. There are special ratios between the lengths of the sides in isosceles right triangles (45°/45°/90° right triangles) and 30°/60°/90° right triangles (right triangles with acute angles of 30° and 60°). As you can see in the first drawing above, the sides of an isosceles right triangle are in a ratio of $x:x:x\sqrt{2}$, with the $x\sqrt{2}$ in the ratio representing the hypotenuse. The sides of a 30°/60°/90° right triangle are in a ratio of $x:x\sqrt{3}:2x$, where $2x$ represents the hypotenuse and x represents the side opposite the 30° angle. (Remember: The longest side has to be opposite the greatest angle.)

Example:

What is the length of the hypotenuse of an isosceles right triangle with legs of length 4?

You can use the Pythagorean theorem to find the hypotenuse, but it's quicker to use the special right triangle ratios. In an isosceles right triangle, the ratio of a leg to the hypotenuse is $x:x\sqrt{2}$. Since the length of a leg is 4, the length of the hypotenuse must be $4\sqrt{2}$.

CHAPTER 6

Triangles and Data Sufficiency

In all Data Sufficiency questions, the approach is to focus on the information you need to answer the question. In geometry, that's often a matter of knowing the correct definition or formula (but not using it!). With triangles, keep in mind the following:

- If you know two angles, you know the third.
- To find the area, you need the base and the height.
- In a right triangle, if you have two sides you can find the third. And if you have two sides, you can find the area.
- In isosceles right triangles and 30°/60°/90° triangles, if you know one side, you can find everything.

Be careful though! Be sure you know as much as you think you do.

Example:

What is the area of right triangle *ABC*?

(1) $AB = 5$

(2) $BC = 4$

Clearly, neither statement alone is sufficient. You may think at first that both together are enough, since it looks like *ABC* is a 3:4:5 right triangle. Not so fast! We're given two sides, but we don't know which sides they are. If *AB* is the hypotenuse, then it is a 3:4:5 triangle, and the area is $\frac{1}{2}(3 \times 4) = 6$, but it's also possible that *AC*, the missing side, is the hypotenuse. In that case, the area would be $\frac{1}{2}(4 \times 5) = 10$. Both statements together are insufficient, and the answer is **(E)**.

GEOMETRY

CHAPTER 6

Quadrilaterals

A **quadrilateral** is a four-sided polygon. Regardless of a quadrilateral's shape, the four interior angles sum to 360°.

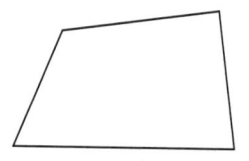

A **parallelogram** is a quadrilateral with two pairs of parallel sides. Opposite sides are equal in length; opposite angles are equal in measure; angles that are not opposite are supplementary to each other (measure of ∠A + measure of ∠D = 180° in the figure below).

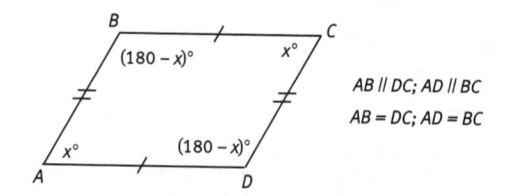

AB ∥ DC; AD ∥ BC
AB = DC; AD = BC

measure of ∠A = measure of ∠C;
measure of ∠B = measure of ∠D

CHAPTER 6

A **rectangle** is a parallelogram with four right angles. Opposite sides are equal; diagonals are equal.

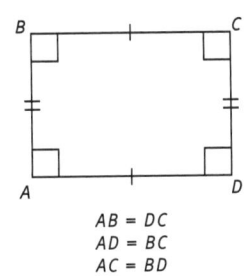

$$AB = DC$$
$$AD = BC$$
$$AC = BD$$

A **square** is a rectangle with equal sides.

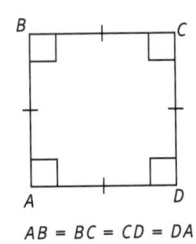

$$AB = BC = CD = DA$$

CHAPTER 6

Perimeters of Quadrilaterals

To find the perimeter of any polygon, you can simply add the lengths of its sides. However, the properties of rectangles and squares lead to simple formulas that may speed up your calculations.

Because the opposite sides are equal, the *perimeter of a rectangle* is twice the sum of the length and the width:

Perimeter = 2(Length + Width)

The perimeter of a 5 by 2 rectangle is 2(5 + 2) = 14.

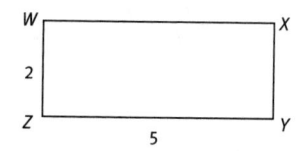

The *perimeter of a square* is equal to the sum of the lengths of the 4 sides. Because all 4 sides are the same length, Perimeter = 4 (Side). If the length of one side of a square is 3, the perimeter is 4 × 3 = 12.

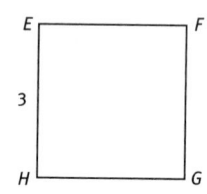

CHAPTER 6

Areas of Quadrilaterals

Area formulas always involve multiplication, and the results are always stated in "square" units. You can see why if you look at the drawing below:

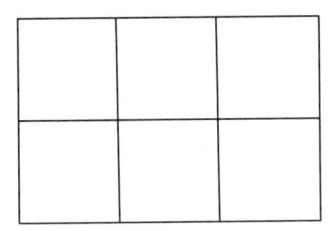

The rectangle is composed of six squares, all equal in size. Let's say that the side of a single small square is 1 unit. Then, we would say that a single square measures "1 by 1." That translates into math as 1×1, or 1^2—in other words, "one square unit."

As you can see from the drawing, there are 6 such square units in the rectangle. That's its area: 6 square units. But you could also find the area by multiplying the number of squares in a row by the number of squares in a column: 3×2, or 6. And since we've defined the length of the side of a square as 1 unit, that's also equivalent to multiplying the length of a horizontal side by the length of a vertical side: again, $3 \times 2 = 6$.

GEOMETRY

CHAPTER 6

Formulas for Area

To find the area of a rectangle, multiply the **length** by the **width**.

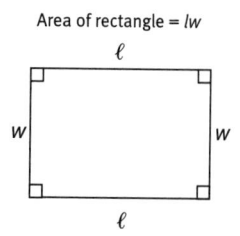

Area of rectangle = *lw*

Since the length and width of a square are equal, the area formula for a square just uses the length of a **side:**

Area of square = (Side)^2 = s^2

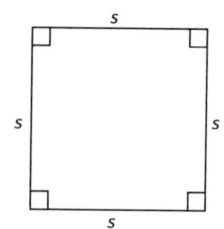

If you're working with a parallelogram, designate one side as the **base**. Then, draw a line segment from one of the vertices opposite the base down to the base so that it intersects the base at a right angle. That line segment will be called the **height**. To find the area of the parallelogram, multiply the length of the base by the length of the height:

Area of parallelogram = (Base)(Height), or $A = bh$

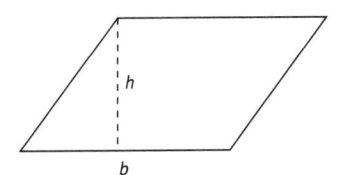

Quadrilaterals and Data Sufficiency

Remember the following:

- In a parallelogram, if you know two adjacent sides, you know all of them; and if you know two adjacent angles, you know all of them.
- In a rectangle, if you know two adjacent sides, you know the area.
- In a square, if you're given virtually any measurement (area, length of a side, length of a diagonal), you can figure out the other measurements.

CHAPTER

6

Circles

Important Terms

Circle: The set of all points in a plane at the same distance from a certain point. This point is called the center of the circle. A circle is labeled by its center point; circle O means the circle with center point O.

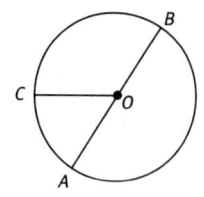

Diameter: A line segment that connects two points on the circle and passes through the center of the circle. AB is a diameter of circle O above.

Radius: A line segment that connects the center of the circle with any point on the circle; *pl.* radii. The radius of a circle is one-half the length of the diameter. In circle O above, OA, OB, and OC are radii.

Central angle: An angle formed by two radii. In circle O above, AOC is a central angle. COB and BOA are also central angles. (The measure of BOA happens to be 180°.) The total degree measure of a circle is 360°.

Chord: A line segment that joins two points on the circle. The longest chord of a circle is its diameter. *AT* is a chord of circle *P* below.

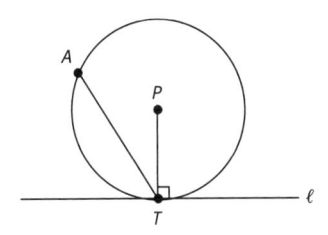

Tangent: A line that touches only one point on the circumference of a circle. A line drawn tangent to a circle is perpendicular to the radius at the point of tangency. In the diagram above, line ℓ is tangent to circle *P* at point *T*.

Circumference and Arc Length

The distance around a polygon is called its **perimeter**; the distance around a circle is called its **circumference**.

The ratio of the circumference of any circle to its diameter is a constant, called **pi** (π). For GMAT purposes, the value of π is usually approximated as 3.14.

Since π equals the ratio of the circumference, *C*, to the diameter, *d*, we can say that $\pi = \dfrac{\text{Circumference}}{\text{Diameter}} = \dfrac{C}{d}$.

The formula for the circumference of a circle is $C = \pi d$.

CHAPTER 6

The circumference formula can also be stated in terms of the radius, r. Since the diameter is twice the length of the radius, that is, $d = 2r$, then $C = 2\pi r$.

An **arc** is a section of the circumference of a circle. Any arc can be thought of as the portion of a circle cut off by a particular central angle. For example, in circle Q, arc ABC is the portion of the circle that is cut off by central angle AQC. Since arcs are associated with central angles, they can be measured in degrees. The degree measure of an arc is equal to that of the central angle that cuts it off. So in circle Q, arc ABC and central angle AQC would have the same degree measure.

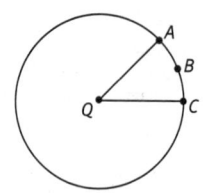

An arc that is exactly half the circumference of its circle is called a **semicircle**.

The length of an arc is the same fraction of a circle's circumference as its degree measure is of 360° (the degree measure of a whole circle). For an arc with a central angle measuring $n°$,

$$\text{Arc length} = \frac{n}{360} (\text{Circumference})$$

$$= \frac{n}{360} \times 2\pi r$$

Example:

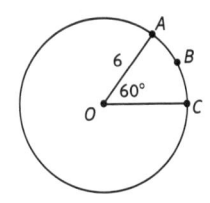

What is the length of arc ABC of circle O above?

$C = 2\pi r$; therefore, if $r = 6$, $C = 2 \times \pi \times 6 = 12\pi$. Since AOC measures 60°, arc ABC is $\frac{60}{360}$, or $\frac{1}{6}$ of the circumference. Thus, the length of arc ABC is $\frac{1}{6} \times 12\pi$, or 2π.

Area and Sector Area Formulas

The area of a circle is πr^2.

A sector is a portion of a circle's area that is bounded by two radii and an arc. The shaded area of circle X is sector AXB.

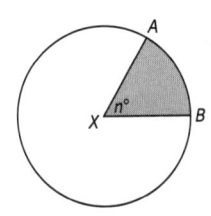

CHAPTER 6

Like arcs, sectors are associated with central angles. And the process and formula used to find the area of a sector are similar to those used to determine arc length. First, find the degree measure of the sector's central angle and figure out what fraction that degree measure is of 360°. Then, multiply the area of the whole circle by that fraction. In a sector whose central angle measures $n°$,

$$\text{Area of sector} = \frac{n}{360} (\text{Area of circle})$$
$$= \frac{n}{360} \pi r^2$$

Example:

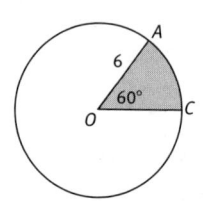

In circle O above, what is the area of sector AOC?

Since $\angle AOC$ measures 60°, a 60° "slice" of the circle is $\frac{60°}{360°}$, or $\frac{1}{6}$ of the total area of the circle. Therefore, the area of the sector is $\frac{1}{6}\pi r^2 = \frac{1}{6}(36\pi) = 6\pi$.

CHAPTER

6

Circles and Data Sufficiency

A circle is a regular shape whose area and perimeter can be determined through the use of formulas. If you're given virtually any measurement (radius, diameter, circumference, area), you can determine all the other measurements.

Example:

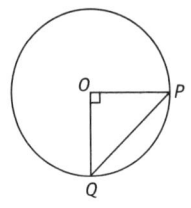

What is the circumference of the circle with center O?

(1) The length of chord $PQ = 4\sqrt{2}$.

(2) The area of sector OPQ is 4π.

To find the circumference, we need the radius, which is either OP or OQ in this circle. Statement (1) gives us the length of PQ. PQ is a chord of the circle (it connects two points on the circle), but it's also the hypotenuse of right triangle OPQ. Do we know anything else about that triangle? Since OP and OQ are both radii of the circle, they must have the same length, so the triangle is an isosceles right triangle. That means that knowing the hypotenuse tells us the length of each leg, which gives us the radius, and is enough to tell us the circumference. Statement (1) is sufficient.

GEOMETRY

CHAPTER 6

Statement (2) gives us the area of the sector. Since the angle at *O* is a right angle, we know that the sector must be one-quarter of the whole circle. Therefore, knowing the area of the sector can give us the area of the whole circle, and from that we can find the radius, and then the circumference. Statement (2) is also sufficient, and the correct answer is **(D)**.

CHAPTER

6

Coordinate Geometry

In coordinate geometry, the locations of points in a plane are indicated by ordered pairs of real numbers.

Important Terms and Concepts

Plane: A flat surface that extends indefinitely in any direction.

x-axis and y-axis: The horizontal (x) and vertical (y) lines that intersect perpendicularly to indicate location on a coordinate plane. Each axis is a number line.

Ordered pair: Two numbers or quantities separated by a comma and enclosed in parentheses. An example would be (8, 7). All the ordered pairs that you'll see in GMAT coordinate geometry problems will be in the form (x, y), where the first quantity, x, tells you how far the point is to the left or right of the y-axis, and the second quantity, y, tells you how far the point is above or below the x-axis.

Coordinates: The numbers that designate distance from an axis in coordinate geometry. The first number is the x-coordinate; the second is the y-coordinate. In the ordered pair (8, 7), 8 is the x-coordinate and 7 is the y-coordinate.

Origin: The point where the x- and y-axes intersect; its coordinates are (0, 0).

CHAPTER

6

Plotting Points

Here's what a coordinate plane looks like:

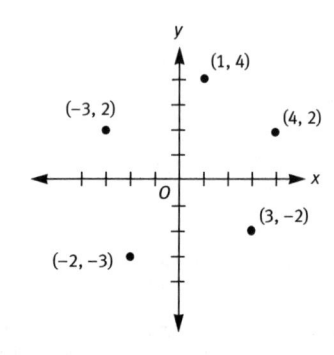

Any point in a coordinate plane can be identified by an ordered pair consisting of its *x*-coordinate and its *y*-coordinate. Every point that lies on the *x*-axis has a *y*-coordinate of 0, and every point that lies on the *y*-axis has an *x*-coordinate of 0.

When you start at the origin and move:

to the right	*x* is positive
to the left	*x* is negative
up	*y* is positive
down	*y* is negative

CHAPTER 6

Therefore, the coordinate plane can be divided into four quadrants, as shown below.

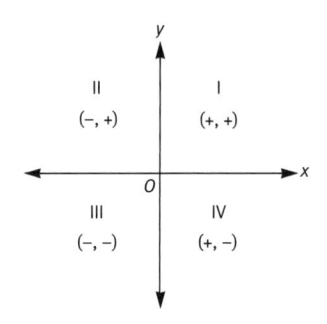

```
         y
         |
   II    |    I
 (−, +)  |  (+, +)
         |
─────────O─────────→ x
         |
   III   |   IV
 (−, −)  |  (+, −)
         |
         ↓
```

Distances on the Coordinate Plane

The distance between two points is equal to the length of the straight-line segment that has those two points as endpoints.

If a line segment is parallel to the x-axis, the y-coordinate of every point on the line segment will be the same. Similarly, if a line segment is parallel to the y-axis, the x-coordinate of every point on the line segment will be the same.

Therefore, to find the length of a line segment parallel to one of the axes, all you have to do is find the difference between the endpoint coordinates that do change. In the diagram below, the length of AB equals $x_2 − x_1$.

GEOMETRY

CHAPTER 6

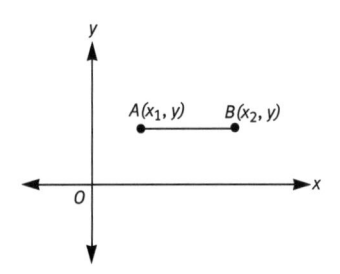

You can find the length of a line segment that is not parallel to one of the axes by treating the line segment as the hypotenuse of a right triangle. Simply draw in the legs of the triangle parallel to the two axes. The length of each leg will be the difference between the x- or y-coordinates of its endpoints. Once you've found the lengths of the legs, you can use the Pythagorean theorem to find the length of the hypotenuse (the original line segment).

In the diagram below, $(DE)^2 = (EF)^2 + (DF)^2$.

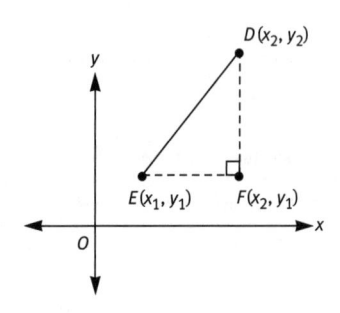

CHAPTER 6

Example:

If the coordinates of point A are (3, 4), and the coordinates of point B are (6, 8), what is the distance between points A and B?

You don't have to draw a diagram to use the method just described, but drawing one may help you to visualize the problem. Plot points A and B and draw in line segment AB. The length of AB is the distance between the two points. Now draw a right triangle, with AB as its hypotenuse. The missing vertex will be the intersection of a line segment drawn through point A parallel to the x-axis and a line segment drawn through point B parallel to the y-axis. Label the point of intersection C. Since the x- and y-axes are perpendicular to each other, AC and BC will also be perpendicular to each other.

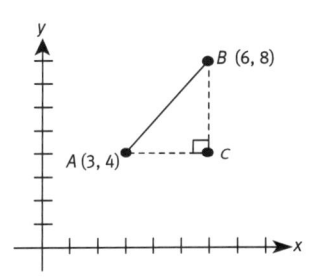

Point C will also have the same x-coordinate as point B and the same y-coordinate as point A. That means that point C has coordinates (6, 4).

To use the Pythagorean theorem, you'll need the lengths of AC and BC. The distance between points A and C is simply the difference between their x-coordinates, while the distance between points B and C is the difference between their

GEOMETRY

CHAPTER 6

y-coordinates. So $AC = 6 - 3 = 3$, and $BC = 8 - 4 = 4$. If you recognize these as the legs of a 3:4:5 right triangle, you'll know immediately that the distance between points A and B must be 5. Otherwise, you'll have to use the Pythagorean theorem to come to the same conclusion.

Equations of Lines

Straight lines can be described by linear equations.

Commonly:

$$y = mx + b,$$

where m is the slope $\left(\dfrac{\Delta y}{\Delta x}\right)$ and b is the point where the line intercepts the y-axis.

Lines that are parallel to the x-axis have a slope of zero and therefore have the equation $y = b$. Lines that are parallel to the y-axis have the equation $x = a$, where a is the x-intercept of that line.

If you're comfortable with linear equations, you'll sometimes want to use them to find the slope of a line or the coordinates of a point on a line. However, many such questions can be answered without determining or manipulating equations. Check the answer choices to see if you can eliminate any by common sense.

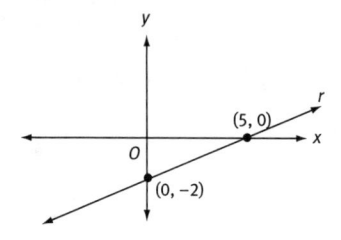

CHAPTER 6

Example:

Line *r* is a straight line as shown above. Which of the following points lies on line *r*?

- ○ (6, 6)
- ○ (7, 3)
- ○ (8, 2)
- ○ (9, 3)
- ○ (10, 2)

Line *r* intercepts the *y*-axis at (0, −2), so you can plug −2 in for *b* in the slope-intercept form of a linear equation. Line *r* has a rise (Δy) of 2 and a run (Δx) of 5, so its slope is $\frac{2}{5}$. That makes the slope-intercept form $y = \frac{2}{5}x - 2$.

The easiest way to proceed from here is to substitute the coordinates of each answer choice into the equation in place of *x* and *y*; only the coordinates that satisfy the equation can lie on the line. Choice **(E)** is the best answer to start with, because 10 is the only *x*-coordinate that will not create a fraction on the right side of the equals sign. Plugging in (10, 2) for *x* and *y* in the slope-intercept equation gives you $2 = \frac{2}{5}(10) - 2$ which simplifies to $2 = 4 - 2$.

That's true, so the correct answer choice is **(E)**.

GEOMETRY

CHAPTER 6

Solids

Important Terms

Solid: A three-dimensional figure. The dimensions are usually called length, width, and height (ℓ, w, and h) or height, width, and depth (h, w, and d). There are only two types of solids that appear with any frequency on the GMAT: rectangular solids (including cubes) and cylinders.

Uniform solid: A solid that could be cut into congruent cross sections (parallel "slices" of equal size and shape) along a given axis. Solids you see on the GMAT will almost certainly be uniform solids.

Face: The surface of a solid that lies in a particular plane. Hexagon *ABCDEF* is one face of the solid pictured below.

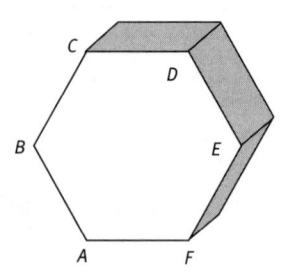

Edge: A line segment that connects adjacent faces of a solid. The sides of hexagon *ABCDEF* are also edges of the solid pictured above.

Base: The "bottom" face of a solid as oriented in any given diagram.

CHAPTER 6

Rectangular solid: A solid with six rectangular faces. All edges meet at right angles. Examples of rectangular solids are cereal boxes, bricks, etc.

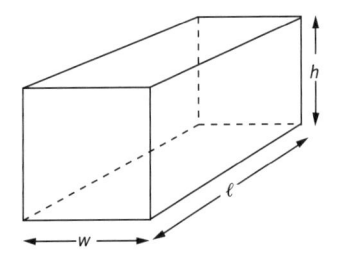

Cube: A special rectangular solid in which all edges are of equal length, e, and therefore all faces are squares. Sugar cubes and dice without rounded corners are examples of cubes.

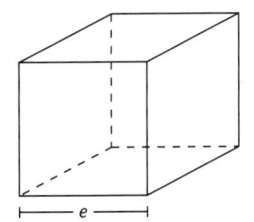

CHAPTER 6

Cylinder: A uniform solid whose horizontal cross section is a circle—for example, a soup can or a pipe that is closed at both ends. A cylinder's measurements are generally given in terms of its radius, r, and its height, h.

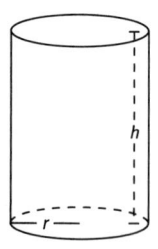

Lateral surface of a cylinder: The "pipe" surface, as opposed to the circular "ends." The lateral surface of a cylinder is unlike most other surfaces of solids that you'll see on the GMAT, first because it does not lie in a plane and second because it forms a closed loop. Think of it as the label around a soup can. If you could remove it from the can in one piece, you would have an open tube. If you then cut the label and unrolled it, it would form a rectangle with a length equal to the circumference of the circular base of the can and a height equal to that of the can.

CHAPTER 6

Formulas for Volume and Surface Area

Volume of a rectangular solid = (Area of base)(Height) = (Length × Width)(Height) = lwh

Surface area of a rectangular solid = Sum of areas of faces = $2lw + 2lh + 2hw$

Since a cube is a rectangular solid for which $l = w = h$, the formula for its volume can be stated in terms of any edge:

- Volume of a cube = lwh = (Edge)(Edge)(Edge) = e^3
- Surface area of a cube = Sum of areas of faces = $6e^2$

To find the volume or surface area of a cylinder, you'll need two pieces of information: the height of the cylinder and the radius of the base.

- Volume of a cylinder = (Area of base)(Height) = $\pi r^2 h$
- Lateral surface area of a cylinder = (Circumference of base)(Height) = $2\pi rh$
- Total surface area of a cylinder = Areas of circular ends + Lateral surface area = $2\pi r^2 + 2\pi rh$

GEOMETRY

CHAPTER

6

Multiple Figures

Some GMAT geometry problems involve combinations of different types of figures. Besides the basic rules and formulas that you would use on normal geometry problems, you'll need an intuitive understanding of how various geometrical concepts relate to each other to answer these "multiple figures" questions correctly. For example, you may have to revisualize the side of a rectangle as the hypotenuse of a neighboring right triangle, or as the diameter of a circumscribed circle. Keep looking for the relationships between the different figures until you find one that leads you to the answer.

Area of Shaded Regions

A common multiple figures question involves a diagram of a geometrical figure that has been broken up into different, irregularly shaped areas, often with one region shaded. You'll usually be asked to find the area of the shaded (or unshaded) portion of the diagram. Your best bet will be to take one of the following two approaches:

1. Break the area into smaller pieces whose separate areas you can find; add those areas together.
2. Find the area of the whole figure; find the area of the region(s) that you're *not* looking for; subtract the latter from the former.

Example:

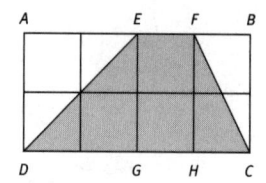

Rectangle *ABCD* above has an area of 72 and is composed of 8 equal squares. What is the area of the shaded region?

CHAPTER 6

The first thing you have to realize is that, for the 8 equal squares to form a total area of 72, each square must have an area of 72 ÷ 8, or 9. Since the area of a square equals the square of the length of a side, each side of a square in the diagram must have a length of $\sqrt{9}$ or 3.

At this point, you choose your approach. Either one will work:

Approach 1:

Break up the shaded area into right triangle *DEG*, rectangle *EFHG*, and right triangle *FHC*. The area of triangle *DEG* is $\frac{1}{2}(6)(6) = 18$. The area of rectangle *EFHG* is (3)(6), or 18. The area of triangle *FHC* is $\frac{1}{2}(3)(6)$, or 9. The total shaded area is 18 + 18 + 9, or 45.

Approach 2:

The area of unshaded right triangle *AED* is $\frac{1}{2}(6)(6)$, or 18. The area of unshaded right triangle *FBC* is $\frac{1}{2}(3)(6)$, or 9. Therefore, the total unshaded area is 18 + 9 = 27. Subtract the total unshaded area from the total area of rectangle *ABCD*: 72 − 27 = 45.

CHAPTER 6

Inscribed/Circumscribed Figures

A polygon is inscribed in a circle if all the vertices of the polygon lie on the circle. A polygon is circumscribed about a circle if all the sides of the polygon are tangent to the circle.

Square ABCD is inscribed in circle O. We can also say that circle O is circumscribed about square ABCD.

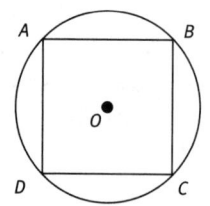

Square PQRS is circumscribed about circle O. We can also say that circle O is inscribed in square PQRS.

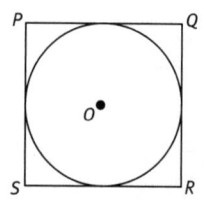

When a triangle is inscribed in a semicircle in such a way that one side of the triangle coincides with the diameter of the semicircle, the triangle is a right triangle.

CHAPTER 6

Example:

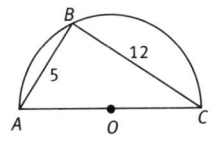

What is the diameter of semicircle O above?

AC is a diameter of semicircle O, because it passes through center point O. So triangle ABC fits the description given above of a right triangle. Moreover, triangle ABC is a special 5:12:13 right triangle with a hypotenuse of 13. Therefore, the length of diameter AC is 13.

CHAPTER 7

OTHER TOPICS

CHAPTER

7

Dealing with Word Problems

The key to solving word problems is translation: turning English into math. Rather than having an equation set up for you, *you* have to decide what arithmetic or algebraic operations to perform on which numbers.

For example, suppose the core of a problem involves working with the equation $3j = s - 4$.

In a word problem, this might be presented as "If John had three times as many macaroons as he has now, he would have four fewer macaroons than Susan would."

Your job is to translate the problem from English into math. A phrase like "three times as many as John has" can be translated as $3j$; the phrase "four fewer than Susan" can be translated as "$s - 4$."

Many people dislike word problems. But on the GMAT, the math involved is often easier than in other math problems. Once you've translated the language, most word problems boil down to rather simple mathematical concepts and processes—probably because the testmakers figure that the extra step of translation makes the problem difficult enough.

Here's a general approach to any word problem:

1. Read through the whole question once, without lingering over details, to get a sense of the overall problem.

2. Identify and label the variables or unknowns in a way that makes it easy to remember what they stand for.

3. Translate the problem into one or more equations, sentence by sentence. Be careful of the order in which you translate the terms. For example, consider the phrase "5 less than $4x$ equals 9." The *correct* way to translate it is: "$4x - 5 = 9$." But many students make the mistake of writing the terms in the order in which they appear in words: "$5 - 4x = 9$."

CHAPTER 7

4. Solve the equation(s).
5. Check your work, if time permits.

Translation Table

This table contains common phrases used in GMAT math problems. The left column lists words and phrases that occur frequently; the right column lists the corresponding algebraic symbols.

Equals, is, was, will be, has, costs, adds up to, is the same as	=
Times, of, multiplied by, product of, twice, double, half, triple	×
Divided by, per, out of, each, ratio of _ to _	÷
Plus, added to, sum, combined, and, total	+
Minus, subtracted from, less than, decreased by, difference between	−
What, how much, how many, a number	Variable (x, n, etc.)

Example:

Beatrice has three dollars more than twice the number of dollars Allan has.

Translate into $B = 3 + 2A$.

OTHER TOPICS

CHAPTER 7

For Word Problems:

Add...

- when you are given the amounts of individual quantities and asked to find the total.

Example:

If the sales tax on a $12.00 lunch is $1.20, what is the total amount of the check?

$$\$12.00 + \$1.20 = \$13.20$$

- when you are given an original amount and an increase, and then asked to find the new amount.

Example:

The bus fare used to be 55 cents. If the fare increased by 35 cents, what is the new fare?

$$55 \text{ cents} + 35 \text{ cents} = 90 \text{ cents}$$

Subtract...

- when you are given the total and one part of the total, and you want to find the remaining part or parts.

Example:

If 32 out of 50 children are girls, what is the number of boys?

$$50 \text{ children} - 32 \text{ girls} = 18 \text{ boys}$$

- when you are given two numbers and asked *how much more* or *how much less* one number is than the other. The amount is called the **difference**.

Example:

How much larger than 30 is 38?

$$38 \text{ (larger)} - 30 \text{ (smaller)} = 8$$

Multiply...

- when you are given an amount for *one* item and asked for the total amount of *many* of these items.

Example:

If 1 book costs $6.50, what is the cost of 12 copies of the same book?

$$12 (\$6.50) = \$78.00$$

Divide...

- when you are given a total amount for *many* items and asked for the amount for *one* item.

Example:

If 5 pounds of apples cost $6.75, what is the price of 1 pound of apples?

$$\$6.75 \div 5 = \$1.35$$

CHAPTER 7

- when you are given the size of one group and the total size for many such identical groups and asked how many of the small groups fit into the larger one.

Example:

How many groups of 30 students can be formed from a total of 240 students?

$$240 \div 30 = 8 \text{ groups of 30 students}$$

Special Word Problems Tip #1

Don't try to combine several sentences into one equation; each sentence usually translates into a separate equation.

Special Word Problems Tip #2

Pay attention to what the question asks for and make a note to yourself if it is not one of the unknowns in the equation(s). Otherwise, you may stop working on the problem too early.

CHAPTER 7

Logic Problems

You won't always have to set up an equation to solve a word problem. Some of the word problems you'll encounter on the GMAT won't fall into recognizable textbook categories. Many of these problems are designed to test your analytical and deductive logic. You can solve them with common sense and a little basic arithmetic. Ask yourself how it would be helpful to arrange the information, such as by drawing a diagram or making a table.

In these problems, the issue is not so much translating English into math as simply using your head. The problem may call for nonmath skills, including the ability to organize and keep track of different possibilities, the ability to visualize something (for instance, the reverse side of a symmetrical shape), the ability to think of the exception that changes the answer to a problem, or the ability to deal with overlapping groups.

Example:

If ! and ∫ are digits, and (! !)(∫ ∫) = 60∫, what is the value of ∫?

Since the symbols used each represent a digit 0 through 9, we know that the product of the multiplication equals a value from 600 to 609. We know that the two quantities multiplied each consist of a two-digit integer in which both digits are the same. So list the relevant two-digit integers (00, 11, 22, 33, 44, 55, 66, 77, 88, and 99), and see which two of them can be multiplied evenly into the 600 to 609 range. Only (11)(55) satisfies this requirement. The ∫ symbol equals 5.

OTHER TOPICS

CHAPTER

7

Tables, Graphs, and Charts

Some questions combine numbers and text with visual formats. Different formats are suitable for organizing different types of information. The formats that appear most frequently on GMAT math questions are tables, bar graphs, line graphs, and pie charts.

Questions involving tables, graphs, and charts may *look* different from other GMAT math questions, but the ideas and principles are the same. The problems are unusual only in the way that they present information, not in what they ask you to do with that information. Typically, they test your ability to work with percents and averages and your ability to solve for unknowns.

Tables

The most basic way to organize information is to create a table. Tables are in some ways the most accurate graphic presentation format—the only way you can misunderstand a number is to read it from the wrong row or column—but they don't allow the reader to spot trends or extremes very readily.

Here's an example of a very simple table.

| John's Income: 2007–2011 ||
YEAR	INCOME
2007	$20,000
2008	$22,000
2009	$18,000
2010	$15,000
2011	$28,000

CHAPTER

7

An easy question might ask for John's income in a particular year or for the difference in his income between two years. To find the difference, you would simply look up the amount for both years and subtract the smaller income from the larger income. A harder question might ask for John's average annual income over the five-year period shown; to determine the average, you would have to find the sum of the five annual incomes and divide it by 5.

Bar Graphs

Here's the same information that you saw previously in a table. This time, it's presented as a bar graph.

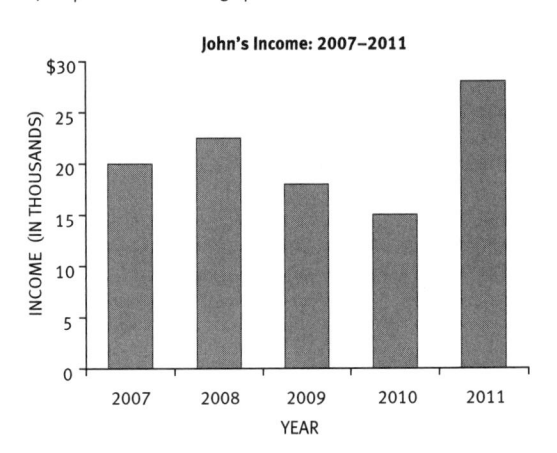

John's Income: 2007–2011

[Bar graph showing John's income in thousands of dollars for years 2007 through 2011. 2007: ~$20K, 2008: ~$22.5K, 2009: ~$18K, 2010: ~$15K, 2011: ~$28K. Y-axis: INCOME (IN THOUSANDS), X-axis: YEAR]

Bar graphs can be used to visually show information that would otherwise appear as numbers in a table. Bar graphs are somewhat less accurate than tables, but that's not necessarily a bad attribute, especially on the GMAT, where estimating often saves time on calculations.

OTHER TOPICS

CHAPTER 7

What's handy about a bar graph is that you can see which values are larger or smaller without reading actual numbers. Just a glance at this graph shows that John's 2011 income was almost double his 2010 income. Numbers are represented on a bar graph by the heights or lengths of the bars. To find the height of a vertical bar, look for the point where a line drawn across the top of the bar parallel to the horizontal axis would intersect the vertical axis. To find the length of a horizontal bar, look for the point where a line drawn across the end of the bar parallel to the vertical axis would intersect the horizontal axis.

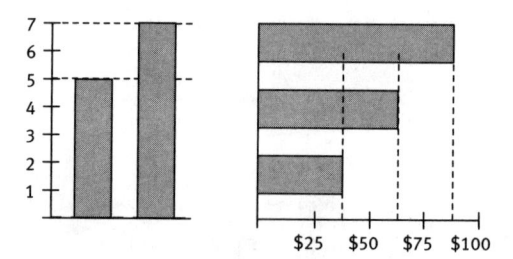

If the height or length of the bar falls in between two numbers on the axis, you will have to estimate.

CHAPTER 7

Line Graphs

Line graphs follow the same general principle as bar graphs, except that instead of using the lengths of bars to represent numbers, they use points connected by lines. The lines further emphasize the relative values of the numbers.

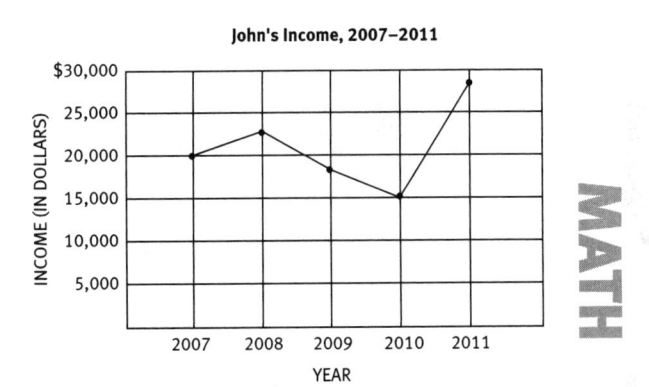

John's Income, 2007–2011

To read John's income for any particular year from this line graph, determine where a line drawn from the appropriate point would intersect the vertical axis.

Pie Charts

Pie charts show how things are distributed: The fraction of a circle occupied by each piece of the "pie" indicates what fraction of the whole that piece represents. In most pie charts, the percentage of the pie occupied by each "slice" will be shown on the slice itself or, for very narrow slices, outside the circle with an arrow or a line pointing to the appropriate slice.

CHAPTER 7

The total size of the whole pie is usually given at the top or bottom of the graph, either as "TOTAL = xxx" or as "100% = xxx." To find the approximate amount represented by a particular piece of the pie, just multiply the whole by the appropriate percent.

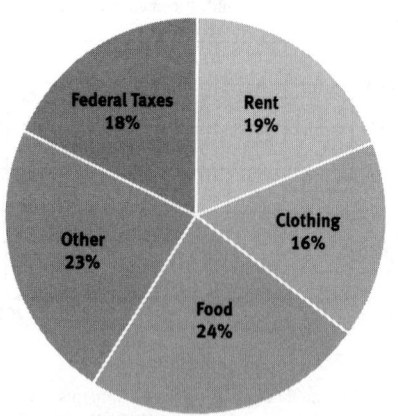

John's Expenditures, 2007
Total = $20,000

- Federal Taxes 18%
- Rent 19%
- Clothing 16%
- Food 24%
- Other 23%

For instance, to find the total tax that John paid to the federal government in 2007, look at the slice of this chart labeled "Federal Tax." It represents 18% of John's 2007 expenditures. Since his total 2007 expenditures were $20,000, he paid 0.18($20,000) = $3,600 in federal taxes in 2007.

One important note about pie charts: If you're not given the whole, and you don't know both the percentage and the actual number that at least one slice represents, you won't be able to find the whole. Pie charts are ideal for presenting the kind of information that ratio problems present in words.

CHAPTER 8

SENTENCE STRUCTURE

CHAPTER 8

The fundamental principles described here will play a role in nearly every Sentence Correction item you see, whether in the original version or among some of the answer choices. Understanding the basic rules of sentence structure enables you to spot the classic GMAT errors quickly. Especially if English is not your native language, be sure to know this basic material.

Complete Sentences

The basic building blocks of sentences are *clauses* and *phrases*.

Phrase: A group of words that does not have a subject and a verb.

Demanding civil rights, more than 200,000 people marched to Washington in 1963.

A penthouse owner might plant a garden *on the roof.*

Ulysses S. Grant, *the Civil War hero and former president,* lost all his money to crooked businessmen.

Clause: A group of words that does contain a subject and a verb. Every sentence contains at least one independent clause; that is, a clause that can stand alone.

More than 200,000 *people marched* to Washington in 1963.

Most sentences contain an independent clause and one or more subordinate clauses—clauses that cannot stand alone. Here the subordinate clause is underlined, and the independent clause is in italics.

<u>Because she was ill</u>, *Mary couldn't attend the play.*

CHAPTER 8

Run-on Sentences

When a sentence consists of more than one clause, those clauses must be joined properly. It is never acceptable to hook two independent clauses together with a comma, as the "sentence" below does. That's called a *run-on sentence*.

Wrong: Nietzsche moved to Basel in 1869, he planned to teach classical philology.

There are a number of acceptable ways to fix a run-on.

1. Make two separate sentences.

    Nietzsche moved to Basel in 1869. He planned to teach classical philology.

2. Change the comma to a semicolon.

    Nietzsche moved to Basel in 1869; he planned to teach classical philology.

3a. Join the two clauses with a coordinating conjunction (usually preceded by a comma).

    Nietzsche moved to Basel in 1869, and he planned to teach classical philology.

The coordinating conjunctions are these:

and   *or*
for   *but*
nor   *yet*

3b. Adverbial conjunctions must be preceded by a period or semicolon.

    Nietzsche planned to teach classical philology; *therefore,* he moved to Basel in 1869.

SENTENCE STRUCTURE

CHAPTER 8

Common adverbial conjunctions are these:

however	*consequently*
then	*nevertheless*
besides	*thus*
hence	*furthermore*
moreover	*otherwise*
therefore	*still*

GRAMMAR

4a. If doing so is appropriate to the meaning, you can join the sentences with a subordinating conjunction.

Because Nietzsche planned to teach classical philology, he moved to Basel in 1869.

There are many subordinating conjunctions. Here are some of the most common ones:

although	*if*
though	*where*
so	*after*
since	*unless*
while	*before*
because	*than*
until	*thereby*

4b. A special kind of subordinate clause is a relative clause. Relative clauses usually begin with *who, that,* or *which,* and they relate the information in one clause to the subject of another clause.

Nietzsche, *who* planned to teach classical philology, moved to Basel in 1869.

CHAPTER 8

Sentence Fragments

Every sentence must contain at least one complete independent clause. If there is no independent clause at all, or if what's supposed to be the independent clause is incomplete, you've got a sentence fragment.

Wrong: While many people, who have worked hard for many years, have not managed to save any money, although they are trying to be more frugal now.

This sentence fragment consists of nothing but subordinate clauses. One of the subordinate clauses must be made into an independent clause.

Correct: Many people, who have worked hard for many years, have not managed to save any money, although they are trying to be more frugal now.

Also Correct: While many people, who have worked hard for many years, have not managed to save any money, they are trying to be more frugal now.

CHAPTER 9

SUBJECT-VERB AGREEMENT

CHAPTER 9

Important Terms and Concepts to Review Before You Read This Section

In English, a subject and its verb must **agree** in number and person. **Number** refers to whether a subject (or a verb) is singular or plural. **Person** refers to first person (*I, we*), second person (*you*), and third person (*he, she, it, one, they*).

Intervening Phrases

When the subject of a sentence is followed by a phrase or relative clause, the phrase or clause is not part of the subject. It simply adds information about that subject.

Learn to recognize groups of words that can come between the subject and verb!

The *prepositional phrase* is an all-time favorite.

Wrong: Wild animals in jungles all over the world is endangered.

The subject of this sentence is *animals,* a plural noun. But the verb, *is,* is singular. The phrase *in jungles all over the world* is distracting for two reasons: (1) It puts distance between the subject and the verb, making it hard to find the subject. (2) It ends with a singular noun, *world,* which looks all right next to the singular verb until you realize that *world* is not the subject.

Correct: Wild animals in jungles all over the world *are* endangered.

CHAPTER 9

Relative clauses are very often placed between a subject and verb.

Wrong: John Clare, who during the mid-nineteenth century wrote many fine poems on rural themes, were confined for decades to an insane asylum.

The subject is *John Clare,* which is singular, but the verb is *were*, which is plural. The fact that the relative clause ends with a plural noun (*themes*) is supposed to distract you from the fact that the subject and verb don't agree.

Correct: John Clare, who during the mid-nineteenth century wrote many fine poems on rural themes, *was* confined for decades to an insane asylum.

Appositives often come between a subject and a verb. Appositives are nouns, pronouns, or noun phrases that are placed next to nouns to further describe them.

Wrong: John Smith, the man who led British expeditions to several American sites, have left several written accounts of dramatic events there.

The subject is *John Smith*, which is singular, but the verb is *have*, which is plural.

Correct: John Smith, the man who led British expeditions to several American sites, *has* left several written accounts of dramatic events there.

SUBJECT-VERB AGREEMENT

CHAPTER 9

A Note about Relative Clauses and Appositives

Some relative clauses and appositives are set off from the rest of the sentence by commas.

> The Geneva Bible, *which was first published in 1560,* was the version of the Bible that Shakespeare knew best.
>
> Johann Sebastian Bach's oldest son, *Johann Christian,* became a distinguished composer in his own right.

When one of these groups of words is set off from the rest of the sentence by commas, it's a dead giveaway that those words are not part of the subject. That makes checking for subject-verb agreement much easier; just ignore the words set off by commas and concentrate on the subject and the verb.

But some relative clauses and appositives, and all prepositional phrases, are not set off by commas.

> The Bible that was first published in Geneva in 1560 was the version of the Bible that Shakespeare knew best.
>
> Johann Sebastian Bach's son Johann Christian became a distinguished composer in his own right.

It's harder to recognize intervening phrases and clauses when they're not set off by commas, but if you remember to check each sentence carefully for such things, you'll be able to pick them out anyway.

CHAPTER 9

Compound Subjects

When two nouns or groups of nouns are joined by *and,* they're called a compound subject and are therefore plural.

Correct: *Ontario and Quebec* contain about two-thirds of the population of Canada.

On the other hand, be careful about what you consider to be a compound subject.

Sometimes nouns joined by *and* do not constitute a plural subject.

Correct: Oatmeal is a high-fiber breakfast.

Also Correct: Ham and eggs is a high-cholesterol breakfast.

The exception to the rule about *and* is this: If two words connected by *and* are thought of as a single unit, they're considered a singular subject. (Hint: If the verb is *is*, look at the word after the verb. If it's singular, the subject is probably singular. For example, in the sentence above, the singular word *breakfast* follows *is*, and that reinforces the conclusion that *ham and eggs* is a singular subject.)

Some connecting phrases may look as though they should make a group of words into a compound subject—but they don't result in a compound subject.

Wrong: George Bernard Shaw, as well as Mahatma Gandhi and River Phoenix, were vegetarians.

And is the only connecting word that results in a compound subject. The following words and phrases **do not** create compound subjects:

> along with as well as
> together with besides
> in addition to

SUBJECT-VERB AGREEMENT

CHAPTER 9

Correct: *George Bernard Shaw,* as well as Mahatma Gandhi and River Phoenix, *was* a vegetarian.

Wrong: Neither Thomas Jefferson nor Alexander Hamilton were supportive of Aaron Burr's political ambitions.

When words in the subject position are connected by *either . . . or* or *neither . . . nor,* the verb agrees with the last word in the pair. If the last word is singular, the verb must be singular. If the last word is plural, the verb must be plural.

Correct: Neither Thomas Jefferson nor Alexander *Hamilton was supportive* of Aaron Burr's political ambitions.

Correct: Neither Thomas Jefferson nor the Federalists *were supportive* of Aaron Burr's political ambitions.

CHAPTER 9

Unusual Sentence Patterns

When you're checking for subject-verb disagreement, remember that the subject doesn't always appear before the verb.

Wrong: There is only a few dozen tigers left in southern China.

A few dozen tigers, plural, is the subject of this sentence, so the verb should also be plural.

Correct: There *are* only a few dozen tigers left in southern China.

Wrong: Dominating the Chicago skyline is the Sears Tower and the John Hancock Building.

The subject of this sentence is a compound subject, *the Sears Tower and the John Hancock Building.* The verb should be plural.

Correct: Dominating the Chicago skyline *are* the Sears Tower and the John Hancock Building.

CHAPTER 9

Subjects That Are Not Nouns or Pronouns

An entire phrase or clause can serve as the subject of a sentence. When used as a subject, a clause always takes a singular verb.

> Whether the economy will improve in the near future *is* a matter of great concern.
>
> That the job market remains tight *is* evident.

Infinitives and gerunds can be used as subjects. Remember that they're singular subjects.

> *To err* is human.
>
> *Rollerblading* is dangerous.

See the section on verbs for more on infinitives and gerunds.

CHAPTER 10

MODIFICATION

CHAPTER 10

Adjectives and adverbs aren't the only modifiers. Phrases and even relative clauses can act as modifiers in a sentence. The following sentence contains several types of modifiers:

> Waiting to regain enough strength to eat, a cheetah, which expends most of its energy in the chase, must rest beside its prey.

Waiting to regain enough strength to eat is a phrase that describes the cheetah. *Which expends most of its energy in the chase* is a relative clause. That also describes the cheetah. *Beside its prey* is another phrase, which modifies the verb *rest*.

If we take *modify* to mean *describe*, then we see the necessity of making the modifiers attach themselves firmly to what they describe. English depends heavily on word order to establish modifying relationships. In other words, most modifiers attach themselves to the first things they can get their hands on in the sentence, even if it's the wrong thing.

Introductory Modifiers

Wrong: Sifting the sand of a riverbed, gold was discovered by prospectors in California in 1848.

A modifying phrase that begins a sentence refers to the noun or pronoun immediately following the phrase. But if we apply that rule here, the sentence says that the *gold was sifting sand*. See the problem? The author clearly meant to say that the prospectors were sifting sand. There are several ways to correct the sentence so that it expresses the intended meaning.

Correct: Sifting the sand in a riverbed, prospectors discovered gold in California in 1848.

CHAPTER

10

Also Correct: Prospectors, sifting the sand in a riverbed, discovered gold in California in 1848.

Also Correct: Gold was discovered by prospectors, who were sifting the sand in a riverbed, in California in 1848.

In all three cases, the phrase or clause directly precedes or follows the noun it describes.

Here's another sentence containing a misplaced modifier.

Wrong: Engraved, printed, and colored by hand, William Blake could make only a few copies of each of his books of poetry.

Our example sentence says that William Blake was engraved, printed, and colored by hand, an unlikely proposition at best. It's clear that the sentence is supposed to say that Blake engraved, printed, and colored his books of poetry by hand and could therefore make only a few copies of each. The sentence can be rewritten to say that.

Correct: William Blake could make only a few copies of each of his books of poetry, which he engraved, printed, and colored by hand.

Notice that when you correct a sentence containing a misplaced modifier, it's sometimes necessary to change the structure of the sentence fairly drastically.

MODIFICATION

CHAPTER
10

Dangling Modifiers

A modifying phrase or clause should clearly refer to a particular word in the sentence. A modifying phrase or clause that does not sensibly refer to any word in the sentence is called a **dangling modifier.** The most common sort of dangler is an introductory modifying phrase that's followed by a word it can't logically refer to.

Wrong: Desiring to free his readers from superstition, the theories of Epicurus are expounded in Lucretius's poem *De rerum natura*.

The problem with this sentence is that the phrase that begins the sentence seems to modify the noun following it: *theories*. In fact, there is really nowhere the modifier can be put to make it work properly, and there is no noun to which it can reasonably refer (*Lucretius's*, the possessive, is functioning as an adjective modifying *poem*.) Get rid of dangling constructions by clarifying the modification relationship or by making the dangler into a subordinate clause.

Correct: Desiring to free his readers from superstition, Lucretius expounded the theories of Epicurus in his poem *De rerum natura*.

Now the phrase *desiring to free his readers from superstition* clearly refers to the proper noun *Lucretius*. Remember, make sure that introductory modifying phrases like the ones in the two previous examples refer to the noun or pronoun that follows the comma.

CHAPTER
10

Other Modifiers

In correcting some of those misplaced introductory modifiers, we move the modifier to a position inside the sentence rather than placing it at the beginning. But modifying phrases inside a sentence can also be misplaced.

Wrong: That night they sat discussing when the cow might calve in the kitchen.

The problem here is the phrase *in the kitchen,* which seems to refer to where the cow might have her calf. The author probably meant to write the following correct sentence:

Correct: That night they sat in the kitchen discussing when the cow might calve.

This sentence is correct because the phrase comes directly after the word it modifies: the verb *sat*.

Wrong: As a young man, the French novelist Gustave Flaubert traveled in Egypt, which was a fascinating experience.

It's not that *Egypt* itself was a fascinating experience, but that traveling there was fascinating.

Correct: Traveling in Egypt as a young man was a fascinating experience for the French novelist Gustave Flaubert.

MODIFICATION

CHAPTER 11

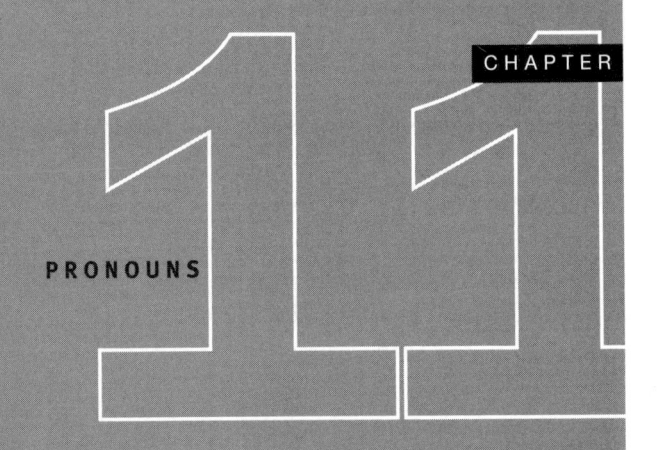

PRONOUNS

CHAPTER 11

Important Terms and Concepts to Review Before You Read This Section

A **pronoun** is a word that is used in place of a noun or another pronoun.

The **antecedent** of a pronoun is the word to which the pronoun refers. The antecedent can precede or follow the pronoun.

> *Henry David Thoreau* went to jail because *he* opposed the Mexican-American War and the Fugitive Slave Act.
>
> Because *he* opposed the Mexican-American War and the Fugitive Slave Act, *Henry David Thoreau* went to jail.

The pronouns you are most likely to see used incorrectly on the exam are the following:

Personal pronouns (Used to refer to people and things.)

I	he	her	us	one
me	she	it	they	
you	him	we	them	

Relative pronouns (Used in relative clauses.)

who	which	where
whom	that	whose

Possessives

my	yours	hers	our	one's
mine	his	their	ours	
your	her	theirs	its	

When doing Sentence Correction questions, always try to locate the antecedent of a pronoun. Most of the pronoun problems you'll encounter on the test result from a problem in the relationship between the pronoun and its antecedent.

CHAPTER

11

Pronoun Reference

In GMAT English, a pronoun must refer clearly to one and only one antecedent.

1. Watch out for sentences in which pronouns refer to indefinite antecedents, paying particular attention to the pronouns *they* and *it*. (Avoid references to some vague *they* or *it*.)

Wrong: *They* serve meals on many of the buses that run from Santiago to Antofagasta. (Who are *they*?)

In this book, *it* says he was a hero.

Correct: Meals are served on many of the buses that run from Santiago to Antofagasta.

This book says he was a hero.

NOTE: It's quite all right to use *it* like this:

It seldom rains in Death Valley.

2. Sometimes a sentence is structured so that a pronoun can refer to more than one thing, and as a result the reader doesn't know what the author intended.

Wrong: Pennsylvania Governor William Keith encouraged the young Benjamin Franklin to open his own printing shop because he perceived that the quality of printing in Philadelphia was poor. (*Which* man perceived that the quality of printing in Philadelphia was poor?)

CHAPTER 11

Pronouns are assumed to refer to the nearest reasonable antecedent. Nonetheless, it is best to avoid structural ambiguity of the sort that occurs in the preceding sentence.

Correct: Because *he* perceived that the quality of printing in Philadelphia was poor, Pennsylvania Governor *William Keith* encouraged the young Benjamin Franklin to open his own printing shop. (*Keith* perceived that the quality of printing was poor.)

Correct: Because the young *Benjamin Franklin* perceived that the quality of printing in Philadelphia was poor, Pennsylvania Governor William Keith encouraged *him* to open *his* own printing shop. (In this version, *Franklin* is the one who perceived that the printing was poor.)

3. Sometimes it's easy to see what the author meant to use for the antecedent, but when you examine the sentence more closely, that antecedent is nowhere to be found. Correct the problem either by replacing the pronoun with a noun or by providing a clear antecedent.

Wrong: To plaster a wall, a mason puts some on a trowel and smoothes it over the laths.

It's clear that the pronoun *some* is intended to refer to the noun *plaster*, but *plaster* occurs in this sentence only in the form *to plaster* (the infinitive). Although infinitives can function as nouns, they describe actions, and in this sentence we need a noun that describes the substance *plaster*.

Better: To plaster a wall, a mason puts some *plaster* on a trowel and smoothes *it* over the laths.

Best: To apply *plaster* to a wall, a mason puts *some* on a trowel and smoothes *it* over the laths.

CHAPTER 11

Wrong: The proslavery writer A. C. C. Thompson questioned Frederick Douglass's authorship of *The Narrative*, claiming that he was too uneducated to have written such an eloquent book.

What's the antecedent of *he*? It should be the noun *Frederick Douglass*, but the sentence contains only the possessive form Douglass's. The possessive form cannot function as the antecedent of a personal pronoun.

Correct: The proslavery writer A. C. C. Thompson questioned whether *Frederick Douglass* actually wrote *The Narrative*, claiming that *he* was too uneducated to have written such an eloquent book.

CHAPTER
11

Oddball Problems

Here are three oddball pronoun-reference problems to watch out for.

Do So

Wrong: It is common for a native New Yorker who has never driven a car to move to another part of the country and have to learn to do it.

Correct: It is common for a native New Yorker who has never driven a car to move to another part of the country and have to learn to *do so*.

One and *You*

When we give advice to others or make general statements, we often use the pronouns *one* and *you*. "You should brush your teeth every day." "One never knows what to do in a situation like that."

It is never acceptable to mix *one* and *you*, or *one* and *yours*, or *your* and *one's* in a sentence together.

Wrong: One shouldn't eat a high-fat diet and avoid exercise and then be surprised when you gain weight.

Correct: *One* shouldn't eat a high-fat diet and avoid exercise and then be surprised when *one* gains weight.

Also Correct: *You* shouldn't eat a high-fat diet and avoid exercise and then be surprised when *you* gain weight.

CHAPTER 11

Also, never use *one* or *one's* to refer to any antecedent except *one*.

Wrong:	A person should leave a light on in an empty house if one wants to give the impression that someone is at home.
Correct:	A *person* should leave a light on in an empty house if *he or she* wants to give the impression that someone is at home.
Also Correct:	*One* should leave a light on in an empty house if *one* wants to give the impression that someone is at home.
Also Correct:	*One* should leave a light on in an empty house if *he or she* wants to give the impression that someone is at home.

The Self Pronouns

Use a *self* pronoun (*myself, yourself,* etc.) only when the antecedent of that pronoun is right there in the sentence.

> Chris hurt *himself* while running.
>
> Karen *herself* was only hurt slightly.

CHAPTER 11

Pronoun Agreement

Always use singular pronouns to refer to singular entities and plural pronouns to refer to plural entities. First, identify the antecedent of a given pronoun—and don't allow yourself to be distracted by a phrase that comes between the two. The GMAT will frequently try to confuse you by inserting a phrase containing plural nouns between a pronoun and its singular antecedent, or vice versa.

Wrong: A cactus will flower in spite of the fact that they receive little water.

Correct: A *cactus* will flower in spite of the fact that *it* receives little water.

Wrong: The number of people with college degrees is many times what they were last summer.

Correct: The *number* of people with college degrees is many times what *it* was last summer.

NOTE: *The number* is always singular. (The number of cookies he ate *was* impressive.) *A number* is always plural. (A number of turkeys *were* gathered outside the shed.)

Pronoun Case

One type of pronoun problem you can't catch by looking at the relationship between a pronoun and its antecedent is a wrong-case problem.

	Subjective Case	Objective Case
First Person:	I, we	me, us
Second Person:	you	you
Third Person:	he, she, it, they, one	him, her, it, them, one
Relative Pronouns:	who, that, which	whom, that, which

When to Use Subjective Case Pronouns

1. Use the subjective case for the subject of a sentence.

    She is falling asleep.

2. Use the subjective case after *is*.

    It is *I*.

3. Use the subjective case in comparisons between the subjects of understood verbs.

    Gary is taller than *I* (am).

CHAPTER 11

GRAMMAR

When to Use Objective Case Pronouns

1. Use the objective case for the object of a verb.
   I called *him*.

2. Use the objective case for the object of a preposition.
   I laughed at *her*.

3. Use the objective case after infinitives and gerunds.
   Asking *him* to go was a big mistake.

4. Use the objective case in comparisons between objects of understood verbs.
   She calls you more than (she calls) *me*.

There probably won't be many times when you are in doubt as to which case of a pronoun is correct. However, the following hints may prove helpful:

When two or more nouns or pronouns are functioning the same way in a sentence, determine the correct case of any pronoun by considering it separately.

Beatrice and (*I* or *me*) are going home early.

Without Beatrice, should the sentence read: *Me am going home early* or *I am going home early*? *I am going*, of course, so the sentence should read: Beatrice and *I* are going home early.

CHAPTER

11

A common mistake in the use of **relative pronouns** is using *who* (subjective case) when *whom* (objective case) is needed, or vice versa. If you tend to confuse the two, try the following system:

> Scholars have disagreed over *whom* is most likely to have written *A Yorkshire Tragedy,* but some early sources attribute it to Shakespeare.

1. Isolate the relative pronoun in its own clause: *whom is most likely to have written A Yorkshire Tragedy.*

2. Ask yourself: *Who* or *whom* wrote *A Yorkshire Tragedy*?

3. Answer with an ordinary personal pronoun: *He* did. (If you are a native speaker of English, your ear undoubtedly tells you that *him did* is wrong.)

4. Since *he* is in the subjective case, we need the subjective case relative pronoun: *who*. Therefore this sentence should read:

    > Scholars have disagreed over *who* is most likely to have written *A Yorkshire Tragedy,* but some early sources attribute it to Shakespeare.

CHAPTER 12

VERBS

CHAPTER 12

Important Terms and Concepts to Review Before You Read This Section

A **verb** is a word that expresses an action or a state of being.

A **verbal** is a word that is formed from a verb but does not function as a verb. There are three kinds of verbals: *participles*, *gerunds*, and *infinitives*.

Participle: Usually ends in *-ing* or *-ed*. It is used as an adjective in a sentence.

> Let *sleeping* dogs lie.
>
> It is difficult to calm a *frightened* child.

Like all verbals, the participle is most frequently found in a phrase.

> *Peering* into his microscope, Robert Koch saw the tuberculosis bacilli.

Gerund: Always ends in *-ing*. It is used in a sentence as a noun.

> *Skiing* can be dangerous.

Note that a gerund can be the subject of a sentence or clause.

> I was surprised at his *acting* like such a coward.

Note from this sentence that a noun or pronoun that comes before a gerund is in the possessive form: *his*, not *him*. The gerund is frequently found in a phrase.

> *Raising a family* is a serious task.

Notice that in this case, the entire phrase functions as the subject of the sentence (that is, *raising a family* takes the place of a noun).

Infinitive: The basic form of a verb, generally preceded by *to*. It is usually used as a noun but may be used as an adjective or an adverb.

It is important to realize that a verbal is not a verb, because a sentence must contain a verb and a verbal won't do. A group of words containing a verbal but lacking a verb is not a sentence.

> Winston Churchill liked *to paint*. (Infinitive used as a noun.)
>
> The will *to conquer* is crucial. (Infinitive used as an adjective—modifies *the will*.)
>
> Students in imperial China studied the Confucian classics *to excel* on civil service exams. (Infinitive used as an adverb—modifies *studied*.)
>
> *To lose* ten pounds is a sensible goal for a dieter. (Note that an infinitive used as a noun can be the subject of a sentence.)

Voice: Active vs. Passive

Occasionally you will be given a choice between an awkward or weak passive construction and an effective active one. The GMAT prefers the active voice unless the passive voice is absolutely necessary.

Poor: A cabin was built near Walden Pond by Henry David Thoreau in 1845. (The subject, *cabin*, is acted upon.)

Better: Henry David Thoreau *built a cabin* near Walden Pond in 1845. (The subject, *Thoreau*, does something.)

The passive voice is formed by taking the object of an active construction and making it the subject of a passive one. The original subject of the active sentence either becomes part of a prepositional phase or is dropped altogether.

CHAPTER

12

Verb Tense

On the GMAT you'll find items that are wrong because a verb is in the wrong tense. To spot this kind of problem, you need to be familiar with both the way each tense is used individually and the ways the tenses are used together.

Present Tense

Use the present tense to describe a state or action occurring in the present time.

> Congress *is* debating health policy this session.

Use the present tense to describe habitual action.

> Many Americans *jog* every day.

Use the present tense to describe "general truths"—things that are always true.

> The earth *is* round and *rotates* on its axis.
>
> Grass *is* green, and the sky *is* blue.

Past Tense

Use the simple past tense to describe an event or state that took place at a specific time in the past and is now over and done with.

> Few people *bought* new cars last year.

There are two other ways to express past action.

> Bread *used to* cost a few cents per loaf.
>
> The president *did promise* not to raise taxes.

CHAPTER **12**

Future Tense

Use the future tense for intended actions or actions expected in the future.

> The twenty-second century *will begin* in the year 2101.

We often express future actions with the expression *to be going to*.

> I *am going to move* to another apartment as soon as possible.

The simple present tense is also used to speak of future events. This is called the *anticipatory future*. We often use the anticipatory future with verbs of motion such as *come, go, arrive, depart,* and *leave*.

> The flight *arrives* at 7:30 tomorrow morning.
>
> The senator *is leaving* for Europe tomorrow.

We also use the anticipatory future in two-clause sentences when one verb is in the regular future tense.

> By the time the bibliography *is* completed, it will already be obsolete.
>
> The disputants will announce the new truce as soon as they *agree* on its terms.

Present Perfect Tense

Use the present perfect tense for actions and states that started in the past and continue into the present time.

> Hawaii *has been* a state since 1959.
>
> Britain *has* not always *been* an island.

VERBS

CHAPTER 12

Use the present perfect for actions and states that happened a number of times in the past and may happen again in the future.

> The Modern Language Association *has awarded* a prize for independent scholars every year since 1983.

Use the present perfect for something that happened at an unspecified time in the past. Notice the difference in meaning between the following two sample sentences:

Present Perfect: Susan Sontag *has written* a critical essay about Leni Riefenstahl.

(We have no idea when—we just know she wrote it.)

Simple Past: Susan Sontag *wrote* a critical essay about Leni Riefenstahl in 1974.

(We use the simple past because we're specifying when Sontag wrote the essay. We wouldn't say: Susan Sontag *has written* a critical essay about Leni Riefenstahl in 1974.)

Past Perfect Tense

The past perfect tense is used to represent past actions or states that were completed before other past states or actions. The more recent past event is expressed in the simple past, and the earlier past event is expressed in the past perfect.

> After he came to America, Vladimir Nabokov translated novels that *he had* written in Russian while he was living in Europe.

Note the difference in meaning between these two sentences:

> The Civil War *had ended* when Lincoln was shot. = *The war was over by the time of the shooting.*

> The Civil War *ended* when Lincoln was shot. = *The war ended at the moment when Lincoln was shot.*

Future Perfect Tense

Use the future perfect tense for a future state or event that will take place before another future event.

> By the time the next election is held, the candidates *will have debated* at least once.

(Note that the anticipatory future is used in the first clause.)

CHAPTER

12

Sequence of Tenses

When a sentence has two or more verbs in it, you should always check to see whether the tenses of those verbs correctly indicate the order in which things happened. As a general rule, if two things happened at the same time, the verbs should be in the same tense.

Wrong: Just as the sun rose, the rooster crows.

Rose is past tense and *crows* is present tense, but the words *just as* indicate that both things happened at the same time. The verbs should be in the same tense.

Correct: Just as the sun *rose*, the rooster *crowed*.

Also Correct: Just as the sun *rises*, the rooster *crows*.

When we're talking about the past or the future, we often want to indicate that one thing happened or will happen before another. That's where the past perfect and the future perfect tenses come in.

Use the past perfect for the earlier of two past events and the simple past for the later event.

Wrong: Mozart finished about two-thirds of the *Requiem* when he died.

Putting both verbs of the sentence in the simple past tense makes it sound as if Mozart wrote two-thirds of the *Requiem* after dying. If we put the first verb into the past perfect, though, the sentence makes much more sense.

Correct: Mozart *had finished* about two-thirds of the *Requiem* when he *died*.

NOTE: Occasionally, the GMAT doesn't use the past perfect for the earlier event. The testmakers use a word like *before* or *after* to make the sequence of events clear. You should always look for the past perfect, but if it's not there, you can settle for the simple past with a time word such as *before* or *after*.

Use the future perfect for the earlier of two future events.

Wrong: By the time I write to Leo, he will probably move.

The point the author is trying to get across is not that Leo will move when he gets the letter, but that by the time the letter arrives he'll be living somewhere else.

Correct: By the time I write to Leo, he *will* probably *have moved*.

When you use a participial phrase in a sentence, the action or the situation that phrase describes is assumed to take place at the same time as the action or state described by the verb of the sentence. In other words, if we say...

> *Being* a French colony, Senegal is a Francophone nation.

...we imply (wrongly, in this case) that Senegal is now a French colony. To make it clear that Senegal used to be a French colony and that's why its citizens speak French, we say:

> *Having been* a French colony, Senegal is a Francophone nation.

In other words, we can make the information in the participial phrase refer to an earlier time than does the verb by changing the regular participle to what's called a perfect participle. The name isn't important as long as you remember that the way to do it is to use *having + the past participle*.

VERBS

CHAPTER
12

You can do the same thing with infinitives by replacing the regular infinitive with *to have + the past participle*.

> I'm glad *to meet* you. (I'm glad to be in the process of meeting you right now.)
>
> I'm glad *to have* met you. (I'm glad now that I met you earlier today, last week, or whenever.)

CHAPTER 12

Mood

Important Terms and Concepts to Review Before You Read This Section

Moods: The forms of verbs that reflect the ways the action or condition conveyed by the verb is thought of by the speaker. English has three moods.

Indicative: Represents something as fact. Verbs in the indicative simply make statements.

Robert Burns *wrote* the poem "To a Mouse."

Imperative: Conveys a command—the subject is understood to be *you*.

Remember the Alamo!

Subjunctive: Represents a wish, probability, thought, condition contrary to fact, or requirement.

The subjunctive form *were* is used in statements that express a wish or in situations that are contrary to fact.

I wish I *were* a rich man. (But I'm not.)

If I *were* you, I wouldn't do that. (But I'm not you.)

The *subjunctive of requirement* is used after verbs such as *ask, demand, insist,* and *suggest*—or after expressions of requirement, suggestion, or demand. A subjunctive verb of requirement is in the base form of the verb: the infinitive without *to*.

Airlines insist that each passenger *pass* through a metal detector.

It's extremely important that silicon chips *be made* in a dust-free environment.

CHAPTER

12

Conditional Sentences

Conditional sentences are if-then statements.

> *If* you go, *then* I'll go, too.
>
> *If* I were you, *(then)* I wouldn't do that.

We use conditional sentences when we want to speculate about the results of a particular situation. There are three types of conditional sentences.

Statements of Fact:

> If Boris Yeltsin resigns, there will be unrest in Russia.
>
> If John Milton met Galileo, they probably discussed astronomy.

Contrary to Fact: The situation in the *if* clause never happened, so what is said in the *then* clause is pure speculation.

> Blaise Pascal wrote that if Cleopatra's nose had been shorter, the face of the world would have changed.
>
> Alexander the Great said, "If I were not Alexander, I would want to be Diogenes."

Future Speculation: Some conditional sentences speculate about the future, but with the idea that the situation in the *if* clause is extremely unlikely to happen.

> If Shakespeare's manuscripts were to be discovered, the texts of some of his plays would be less uncertain.

CHAPTER 13

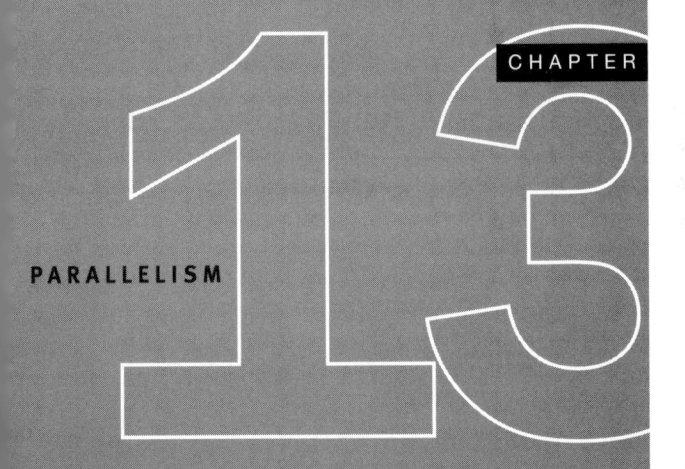

PARALLELISM

CHAPTER 13

Important Terms and Concepts to Review Before You Read This Section

When you express a number of ideas of equal importance and function in the same sentence, you should put them all in the same grammatical form (that is, all nouns, all adjectives, all gerunds, all clauses, or whatever). That's called *parallel structure* or *parallelism*.

Coordinate Ideas

Coordinate ideas occur in pairs or in series, and they are linked by conjunctions like *and, but, or,* and *nor* or, in certain instances, by linking verbs like *is*.

Wrong: To earn credits, an American college student can take up folk dancing, ballet, or study belly dancing.

Correct: To earn credits, an American college student can take up folk *dancing, ballet,* or belly *dancing.*

Once you begin repeating a word in a series, you must follow through.

Wrong: A wage earner might invest her money in stocks, in bonds, or real estate.

Correct: A wage earner might invest her money *in* stocks, *in* bonds, or *in* real estate.

Also Correct: A wage earner might invest her money *in* stocks, bonds, or real estate.

You must either repeat the preposition in front of each element in the series or include it only in front of the first item in the series. Anything else violates the rules of parallelism. This principle applies equally to prepositions (*in, on, by, with,* etc.), articles (*the, a, an*), helping verbs (*had, has, would,* etc.), and possessive pronouns (*his, her,* etc.).

CHAPTER 13

Correlative Constructions

A group of words in English, called *correlative conjunctions*, are used to relate two ideas in some way. Here's a list of them:

> *both . . . and*
>
> *either . . . or*
>
> *neither . . . nor*
>
> *not only . . . but (also)*

You should always be careful to place correlative conjunctions immediately before the terms they're coordinating.

Wrong: Isaac Newton not only studied physics but also theology.

The problem here is that the author intends to coordinate the two nouns *physics* and *theology* but makes the mistake of putting the verb of the sentence (*studied*) after the first element of the construction (*not only*). Note that the solution to an error like this is usually to move one of the conjunctions.

Correct: Isaac Newton studied not only *physics* but also *theology*.

PARALLELISM

CHAPTER

13

Compared or Contrasted Ideas

Frequently, two or more ideas are compared or contrasted within the same sentence. Compared or contrasted ideas should be presented in the same grammatical form.

Certain phrases should clue you in to the fact that the sentence contains ideas that should be presented in parallel form. These phrases include *as . . . as* and *more* (or *less*) x *than* y.

Wrong: Skiing is as strenuous as to run.

Correct: *Skiing* is as strenuous as *running*.

Wrong: Skiing is less dangerous than to rappel down a cliff.

Correct: *To ski* is less dangerous than *to rappel* down a cliff.

CHAPTER

13

To Be

When an infinitive is the subject of the sentence, don't use a gerund after the verb, and vice versa. Pair infinitives with infinitives and gerunds with gerunds.

Wrong: To drive while intoxicated is risking grave injury and criminal charges.

Correct: *To drive* while intoxicated is *to risk* grave injury and criminal charges.

When two clauses express parallel thoughts the way these do, don't use an infinitive to begin one and a gerund to begin the other. Use two infinitives or two gerunds, whichever is idiomatic.

Wrong: Calling someone long-distance is an expensive way to communicate; to send an email is much cheaper.

Correct: *Calling* someone long-distance is an expensive way to communicate; *sending* an email is much cheaper.

Also Correct: *To call* someone long-distance is an expensive way to communicate; *to send* an email is much cheaper.

CHAPTER

13

Active and Passive

Don't put one clause of a sentence in the active voice and one in the passive voice if there's any way to avoid it.

Poor: Richard Strauss wrote *Salome*, and then *Elektra* was composed by him.

Better: Richard Strauss wrote *Salome* and then composed *Elektra*.

CHAPTER 14

COMPARISONS

CHAPTER

14

On the GMAT, you will see a number of sentences that make comparisons. To be considered correct, a sentence that makes a comparison must do two things. First, it must make clear what is being compared, and second, it must compare things that logically can be compared. A sentence that makes an unclear or illogical comparison is grammatically unacceptable.

Quite a few expressions can be used to make comparisons. Here are some of them:

as . . . as	like
more . . . than	unlike
less . . . than	as
similar to	different from

These expressions, and other comparative expressions, should remind you to ask two questions about the comparison in the sentence: Is it clear? Is it logical?

Unclear Comparisons

Sometimes it isn't clear what the author is trying to compare.

Wrong: Byron admired Dryden more than Wordsworth.

There are two ways to interpret this sentence: that Dryden meant more to Byron than Wordsworth did, or that Byron thought more highly of Dryden than Wordsworth did. Whichever meaning you choose, the problem can be cleared up by adding more words to the sentence.

Correct: Byron admired Dryden more than *he did* Wordsworth.

Also Correct: Byron admired Dryden more than *Wordsworth did*.

CHAPTER
14

Illogical Comparisons

Sometimes what the author meant to say is clear enough, but the author ended up actually saying something else.

Wrong: The peaches here are riper than any other fruit stand.

This sentence is comparing *peaches* to *fruit stands*, even though that's clearly not the intention of the author. We can correct it so that we're comparing peaches to peaches by inserting the phrase *those at*.

Correct: The peaches here are riper than *those at* any other fruit stand.

Now the pronoun *those* is standing in for *peaches*, so the sentence is comparing things that can be reasonably compared: the peaches here and some other peaches.

Incomplete comparisons like this one are normally corrected by inserting a phrase like *those of, those in, those at, that of, that in,* and *that at*.

Incomplete comparisons can also be corrected by use of the possessive.

Wrong: Many critics considered Enrico Caruso's voice better than any other tenor. (This is comparing a voice to a person.)

Correct: Many critics considered Enrico Caruso's voice better than *any other tenor's*.

Note that this is a shortened version of the following:

Many critics considered Enrico Caruso's voice better than *any other tenor's* voice.

NOTE: It's perfectly acceptable to leave out the word *voice* at the end of the sentence (see the chapter on Ellipsis).

COMPARISONS

CHAPTER 14

The second sort of incomplete comparison occurs when one thing is being compared to a group it is a part of. This error is corrected by inserting either the word *other* or the word *else*.

Wrong: Astaire danced better than any man in the world.

This is wrong because he couldn't have danced better than himself.

Correct: Astaire danced better than any *other* man in the world.

Comparative Forms

The comparative form is used when comparing only two members of a class, and the superlative is used for three or more.

> Loretta's grass grows *more vigorously* than Jim's.
> Loretta's grass grows the *most vigorously* of any in the neighborhood.
>
> Of Buchanan and Lincoln, the *latter* was *taller*.
> Of McKinley, Roosevelt, and Taft, the *last* was *heaviest*.

CHAPTER 15

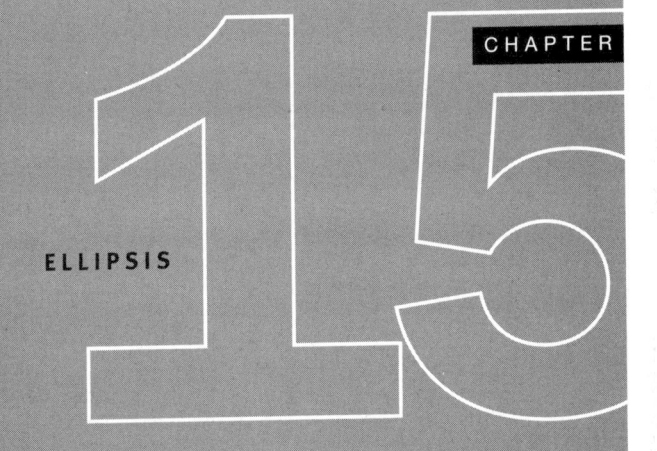

ELLIPSIS

CHAPTER

15

What Is Ellipsis?

Ellipsis: The omission from a sentence of words that are clearly understood. Ellipsis is perfectly acceptable as long as it's done properly—in fact, we do it all the time. Not many people would make a statement like this:

I've seen more movies this year than you have seen movies this year.

Instead, we would automatically shorten the statement so it's much more concise and natural sounding:

I've seen more movies this year than you have.

On the GMAT, though, you may encounter sentences in which the ellipsis has gone just a little too far and essential parts of the sentence have been left out. Sometimes faulty ellipsis is very obvious because it results in an unclear or silly sentence. Remember our unclear comparison?

Wrong: Byron admired Dryden more than Wordsworth.

The problem here, as we mentioned before, is that the meaning of the sentence isn't clear. This is the result of faulty ellipsis—words needed to make the meaning plain have been left out.

Correct: Byron admired Dryden more than *he did* Wordsworth.

Also Correct: Byron admired Dryden more than *Wordsworth did*.

Many times, however, faulty ellipsis isn't so easy to spot. That's because only one small word has been left out of a sentence and, while the meaning is reasonably clear, the sentence is grammatically incorrect. You must learn to watch for prepositions, articles, possessives, and so on that have been incorrectly left out of a sentence. Improper ellipsis often results in an unparallel sentence or an illogical comparison.

CHAPTER

15

In the following sentence, ellipsis is properly used:

> *The Spectator* was written by Addison and Steele.

This is a shorter way of saying the following:

> *The Spectator* was written by Addison and by Steele.

It's all right to leave the second *by* out of the sentence because the same preposition appears before *Addison* and before *Steele,* so you need to use it only once.

Now watch what happens when ellipsis is improperly used.

Wrong: Ezra Pound was interested but not very knowledgeable about economics.

This is wrong because the preposition that's needed after the word *interested (in)* is not the same as the preposition that follows the word *knowledgeable (about)*.

Correct: Ezra Pound was *interested in* but not very *knowledgeable about* economics.

One way to check for faulty ellipsis is to complete each component idea in the sentence. Unless each part of the sentence can stand alone, you've found a case of faulty ellipsis. Trying that with our wrong example, we have this:

Wrong: Ezra Pound was *interested about* economics, but Pound was not very *knowledgeable about* economics.

Clearly that won't do, but both parts of the correct version can stand alone.

ELLIPSIS

CHAPTER 15

Correct: Ezra Pound was *interested in* economics, but Pound was not very *knowledgeable about* economics.

Wrong: London always has and always will be the capital of the United Kingdom.

This is wrong because the verb form that's needed after *has* is not the same as the one that's needed after *will*, so both must be included.

Correct: London *always has been* and *always will be* the capital of the United Kingdom.

Note that in the correct version, both parts of the sentence can stand alone. See what happens if you do that with the wrong version.

CHAPTER 16

STYLE

CHAPTER 16

Redundancy

Using two words or phrases that have exactly the same meaning when one word or phrase would be sufficient to get the point across is called *redundancy*.

Wrong: The school was established and founded by Quakers in 1906.

Established and *founded* both have the same meaning in this sentence: set up, created. One or the other is acceptable—using both results in redundancy.

Correct: The school was *established* by Quakers in 1906.

Correct: The school was *founded* by Quakers in 1906.

Wrong: If temperatures drop during the night and the roads become icy, it is probable that the schools may be closed tomorrow.

Both the phrase *it is probable* and the verb *may* indicate the possibility of closing the schools—using both is redundant.

Correct: If temperatures drop during the night and the roads become icy, it is *probable* that the schools will be closed tomorrow.

Also Correct: If temperatures drop during the night and the roads become icy, the schools *may* be closed tomorrow.

CHAPTER
16

Wordiness

More often than not, having extra words in a sentence isn't repetitious but is still a problem because the thought could be expressed more concisely. Versions of Sentence Correction questions can be unacceptable partly or entirely because they're too wordy; choose shorter versions as long as no essential words have been left out of the sentence.

Wordy: The supply of musical instruments that are antique is limited, so they become more valuable each year.

Better: The supply of *antique musical instruments* is limited, so they become more valuable each year.

Wordy: Barbara Johnson and Alice Walker are in agreement with each other that Zora Neale Hurston was a major writer.

Better: Barbara Johnson and Alice Walker *agree* that Zora Neale Hurston was a major writer.

CHAPTER 17

COMMONLY
MISUSED
WORDS

CHAPTER

17

Idiom

Sometimes the right way to say something is not a matter of grammar but rather of *idiom:* an accepted, set phrase or usage that's right for no other reason than that's just the way we say it.

There are so many different ways to distort idiomatic expressions that we can't possibly show you every "idiom error" and "unidiomatic usage" that you could encounter on the GMAT. We can, however, show you some general types of idiom errors.

Most of what we call idioms are pairs of words that are used together to convey a particular meaning, and many idiom errors result from substituting an unacceptable word—usually a preposition—for a word that is always part of the idiom.

Wrong: Brigitte Bardot has joined an organization that is concerned in preventing cruelty to animals.

The adjective *concerned* is followed by either *about* or *with*, either of which would be idiomatic here. But the expression *concerned in* simply isn't idiomatic—we just don't say it that way.

Correct: Brigitte Bardot has joined an organization that is *concerned with* preventing cruelty to animals.

Also Correct: Brigitte Bardot has joined an organization that is *concerned about* preventing cruelty to animals.

There are many possible idiom errors of this kind. The most frequently tested errors are in the list of commonly misused words at the end of this chapter.

CHAPTER

17

Negatives

You will probably run across at least one item that tests your ability to recognize the difference between idiomatic and unidiomatic ways to express negative ideas. You already know that a double negative is a no-no in standard written English. You wouldn't have any trouble realizing that a sentence such as "I don't want no help," is unacceptable. But the incorrect negatives you will probably see on the exam won't be quite that obvious.

The obviously negative words are these:

neither	nobody	nor
nowhere	never	none
not	no one	nothing

Don't forget that the following words are also grammatically negative:

| barely | rarely | without |
| hardly | seldom | scarcely |

In Sentence Correction questions, you'll find problems with these words where sentences connect two or three negative ideas. Read through the following correct example sentences carefully.

There were *no* threats. There were *no* bombing campaigns.

There were *neither* threats *nor* bombing campaigns.

There were *no* threats or bombing campaigns.

There were *no* threats *and no* bombing campaigns.

There were *no* threats, *nor* were there bombing campaigns.

CHAPTER 17

These are the most common idiomatic ways to join two negative ideas. If you can remember these patterns, you can probably eliminate many wrong answers because they in some way violate these idiomatic patterns.

Wrong: When Walt Whitman's family moved to Brooklyn, there were *no bridges nor tunnels* across the East River.

The phrase *no bridges nor tunnels* is not idiomatic—it contains a double negative. The sentence can be rewritten in several ways to correct the problem.

Correct: There were *no bridges or tunnels* across the East River.

Also Correct: There were *neither bridges nor tunnels* across the East River.

Also Correct: There were *no bridges and no tunnels* across the East River.

Negatives can also cause problems when used in a series. Words like *no*, *not*, and *without* must follow the same rules as prepositions, articles, helping verbs, etc.

Wrong: After the floods in the Midwest, many farmers were left without homes, businesses, and huge bills to replace all they had lost.

When a preposition, such as *without* in this sentence, is used in front of only the first member of a series, it's taken to refer to all three members of the series. Here, that rule causes the sentence to say that the farmers were left without homes, without businesses, and without huge bills to replace what they had lost, which makes no sense. There are several ways to rewrite the sentence so that it makes sense.

CHAPTER 17

Correct: After the floods in the Midwest, many farmers were left *without* homes, *without* businesses, and *with* huge bills to replace all they had lost.

Also Correct: After the floods in the Midwest, many farmers were left *with no* homes, *with no* businesses, and *with* huge bills to replace all they had lost.

Also Correct: After the floods in the Midwest, many farmers were left *with no* homes, *no* businesses, and huge bills to replace all they had lost.

COMMONLY MISUSED WORDS

CHAPTER 17

Other Commonly Misused Words

accept
except

To *accept* is to willingly receive; to *except* is to omit or exclude.

> A student may be *accepted* by a college because, if you *except* a failing grade in one or two courses, his academic record is excellent. (Note: *Except* is usually used as a preposition meaning "with the exception of." In many states, stores are open every day *except* Sunday.)

adapt
adopt

To *adapt* is to change something to make it suitable for a certain purpose; to *adopt* is to make something one's own.

> William Faulkner *adapted* Hemingway's novel *To Have and Have Not* for the movies.

> The Allan family *adopted* Edgar Poe as a child.

affect
effect

As verbs, to *affect* is to influence or change; to *effect* is to cause or to make (something) happen.

> A lack of rainfall usually *affects* the size of a harvest.

> Penicillin *effects* a rapid recovery in most patients with bacterial infections.

(Note: *Effect* is most commonly used as a noun meaning "influence." Illegible signs on a road have a bad *effect* on safety.)

CHAPTER 17

allusion
delusion
illusion

Allusion is an indirect reference; a *delusion* is something that is falsely believed; an *illusion* is a false, misleading, or deceptive appearance.

> Someone who fills his talk with *allusions* to literature and art to create the *illusion* that he is very learned may have *delusions* of grandeur.

among
between

In most cases, you should use *between* for two items and *among* for more than two. There are exceptions, however; *among* tends to be used for less definite or less exact relationships.

> The competition *between* Obama and McCain grew intense.
>
> He is always at his best *among* strangers.
>
> BUT: Plant the trees in the area *between* the road, the wall, and the fence.

amount
number

Amount should be used to refer to a singular or noncountable word, and *number* should be used to refer to a plural or countable word.

> The *amount* of money he carried in his pocket would feed a substantial *number* of people.

COMMONLY MISUSED WORDS

CHAPTER 17

another
the other

Another refers to any other; *the other* is more specific—it refers to one particular other.

> Put *another* log on the fire (any one).
>
> Put *the other* log on the fire (the last one).
>
> The men were passing the specimen from one to *the other* (two men back and forth).
>
> They passed the specimen from one to *another* (three or more).

as
like

Like is a preposition; it introduces a phrase. *As*, when functioning as a conjunction, introduces a subordinate clause.

> Jenny Lind was said to sing *like* a nightingale.
>
> Jenny Lind was said to sing *as* a nightingale sings.

as . . . as

The idiom is *as . . . as*.

> That suit is *as* expensive *as* (NOT *than*) this one.

assure
ensure
insure

To *ensure* is to make certain, safe, or secure; to *insure* is to provide for financial payment in case of loss; to *assure* is to inform positively.

> He *assured* his children that he had *insured* his life to *ensure* that they would not suffer poverty if he died.

CHAPTER 17

because

To say "the reason is because" is considered ungrammatical. Use *that* instead.

> The reason many high schools use metal detectors is *that* some children bring weapons to school.

> Also Correct: Many high schools use metal detectors *because* some children bring weapons to school.

beside
besides

Beside means "next to" something; *besides* means "in addition to."

> The president sat *beside* the Japanese prime minister at the banquet.

> *Besides* the team, reporters often frequent the locker room.

between . . . and

The idiom is *between . . . and.*

> Call *between* five *and* (NOT *to*) six o'clock.

> He chose *between* fish *and* (NOT *or*) meat.

compare to
compare with

To *compare to* is to point out an abstract or figurative likeness; to *compare with* is to consider likenesses and differences in general.

> Shall I *compare* thee *to* a summer's day?

> *Compared with* a summer day, today is cold.

CHAPTER 17

different from

Different is usually used with the preposition *from,* usually not with *than; differ* can also be used with *with*.

> Major's policies were slightly *different from* Thatcher's.
>
> On that issue, I *differ with* you.

each other
one another

Each other is used to refer to two things, and *one another* is used for three or more.

> Those two theories contradict *each other*.
>
> Those three theories contradict *one another*.

eminent
imminent
immanent

Eminent means "prominent, outstanding"; *imminent* means "likely to happen, impending"; *immanent* means "existing within, intrinsic."

> The whole school was excited about the *imminent* arrival of the *eminent* scientist.
>
> Scrooge is characterized by *immanent* selfishness.

fewer
less

Use *fewer* before a plural noun; use *less* before a singular one.

> There are *fewer* apples on this tree than there were last year.
>
> A politician earns *less* money than an executive in the private sector does.

CHAPTER 17

had
would have

Contrary-to-fact and improbable conditional sentences use the helping verb *would* in the *then* clause but never in the *if* clause.

> If Cleopatra's nose *had* been (NOT *would have been*) shorter, the face of the world *would have* changed.

if
whether

In GMAT English, use *if* only in conditional statements.

> I do not know *whether* (NOT *if*) it is true.
>
> BUT: *If* it is true, I am in hot water.

imply
infer

To *imply* is to state or indicate indirectly; to *infer* is to deduce or conclude.

> Pete sarcastically *implied* that he was angry.
>
> Joe *inferred* from Mary's dejected look that she had failed the exam.

ingenious
ingenuous

Ingenious means "intelligent, clever, or resourceful"; *ingenuous* means "innocent, naive, or simple."

> The thief entered the bank vault by means of an *ingenious* magnetic device.
>
> Alice is so *ingenuous* that she refuses to believe that anyone would deliberately do harm.

COMMONLY MISUSED WORDS

CHAPTER 17

maybe

Don't use *maybe* to modify an adjective or another adverb.

> That's a potentially (NOT *maybe*) dangerous thing to do.

regard as

Regard as is the correct idiom; *regard to be* is wrong.

> I *regard* you *as* (NOT *to be*) a close friend.

to be able

Don't use a form of *to be able* preceding the passive form of an infinitive.

> My old television *cannot* (NOT *is not able to*) be repaired.
>
> Also Correct: He is *not able* to repair it.

when
where

Do not use *when* or *where* in a definition or where *that* would be more appropriate.

> A convention is a meeting of people with something in common (NOT *a convention is where a number of people*, etc.).
>
> A diagram is a sketch that illustrates (NOT *is when a sketch is made to illustrate*) the parts of something.
>
> I read that (NOT *where*) you had to leave town.